Carl Reinecke, E. M. Trevenen Dawson

The Beethoven Pianoforte Sonatas

Explained for the Lovers of the Musical Art - Vol. 1

Carl Reinecke, E. M. Trevenen Dawson

The Beethoven Pianoforte Sonatas
Explained for the Lovers of the Musical Art - Vol. 1

ISBN/EAN: 9783337127626

Printed in Europe, USA, Canada, Australia, Japan

Cover: Foto ©Thomas Meinert / pixelio.de

More available books at **www.hansebooks.com**

BEETHOVEN'S PIANOFORTE SONATAS

EXPLAINED FOR THE LOVERS OF THE MUSICAL ART.

BY

ERNST VON ELTERLEIN

With a Preface by E. PAUER.

Translated from the German by
EMILY HILL.

REVISED TRANSLATION FORMING
THE FIFTH EDITION.

LONDON:
WILLIAM REEVES, 185, Fleet Street, E.C.
1898.

ILLUSTRATIONS.

The Portrait of Beethoven as fronting the title is, on the authority of Mr. C. Czerny (Beethoven's most intimate friend), the only correct likeness published of this great man.

Beethoven's House at Bonn, facing page 1.

Printed by
William Reeves, 185, Fleet St.,
London, E.C.

CONTENTS.

	PAGE.
FIRST PART	11

The Sonata in General.

SECOND PART	18

The Sonata before Beethoven.

THIRD PART	30

Beethoven.

FOURTH PART	37

Beethoven's Sonatas.

Op. 2, No. 1. Op. 2, No. 2. Op 2, No. 3. Op. 6. Op. 7. Op. 10, No. 1. Op. 10, No. 2. Op. 10, No. 2. Op. 13. Op. 14, Nos. 1 and 2. Op. 22. Op. 26. Op. 27, No. 1. Op. 27, No. 2. Op. 28. Op. 31, No. 1. Op. 31, No. 2. Op. 31, No. 3. Op. 49, Nos 1 and 2. Op. 53. Op. 54. Op. 57. Op. 78. Op. 79. Op. 81. Op. 90. Op. 101. Op. 106. Op. 109. Op. 110. Op 111.

FIFTH PART	126

Retrospective.

Concluding Remarks.

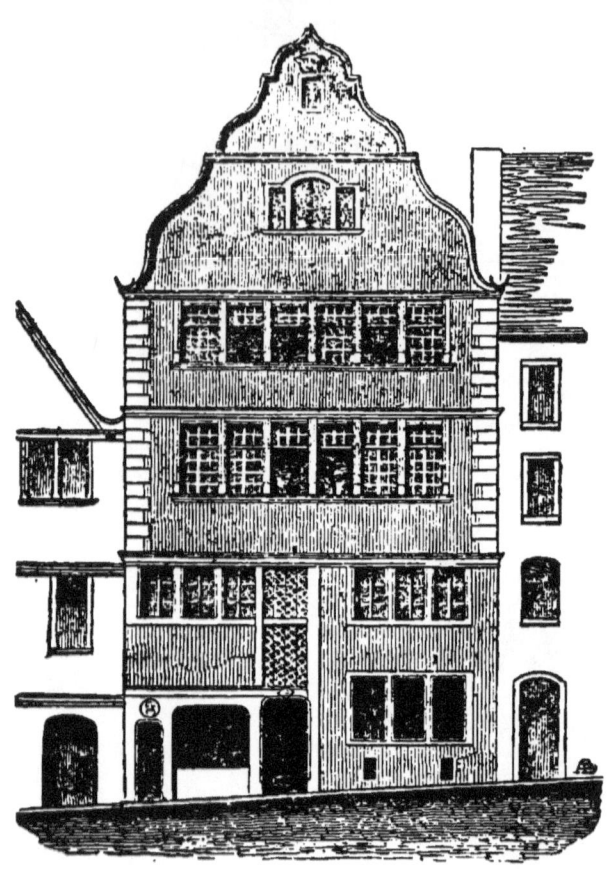

BEETHOVEN'S HOUSE AT BONN.

Beethoven's Pianoforte Sonatas, Explained by Elterlein.

PREFACE TO THE FIRST EDITION OF THE TRANSLATION.

The transcendent beauty and the exceeding importance of Beethoven's Pianoforte Sonatas are facts now universally recognised. It is a healthy sign of musical progress and an undeniable proof of the spread of an improved taste and of a genuine appreciation of the excellent in musical art, that various nations now emulate each other's efforts in issuing correct and excellent editions of these great works. We now possess good and correct editions of Beethoven's Sonatas at such cheap and modest prices, that the entire collection of the thirty-eight Sonatas is to be had for the same price which our grandfathers paid for a single one; and this remarkable reduction of price has undoubtedly contributed in no small degree to the universal popularity which this unrivalled monument of musical art has now everywhere obtained.

To describe the contents of a musical work is always a difficult task; and it cannot be denied that a great deal of nonsense has been written, in the endeavour to analyse, describe and annotate the works of great musical composers. No author has had to suffer more from the indiscreet zeal of busy shallow annotators than Ludwig van Beethoven; no other composer's works have been so unwarrantably and unnecessarily overladen with weak description. The small work, Beethoven's Clavier-Sonaten für Freunde der Tonkunst erläutert von Ernst von Elterlein, stands forth as an honourable exception amidst the host of insipid commentaries on the great master's works—the multudinous explanations that explain nothing. Elterlein's book appeared in Leipsic, in 1856. It has, since that year, gone through many editions, and has obtained great and deserved popularity in Germany. Although Herr von Elterlein is a musical amateur, he writes with the ripe knowledge and thorough understanding of a practical musician; and as the merits of his book speak for themselves, any further praise would be superfluous.

Herr von Elterlein's design is not so much to describe the beauties of Beethoven's Sonatas, as to direct the performer's attention to these beauties, and to point out the leading and characteristic features of each separate piece. It was reserved for Beethoven to give expression, in his Sonatas, to the highest and loftiest feelings of the human heart. In these unapproachable master-pieces, he is not only pathetic, but also sincere, humorous, tender, graceful, simple—in short, he expresses in them every varying shade of feeling that can agitate the human heart. To point out all these varying shades, to indicate to the earnest student of Beethoven all these numberless beauties, is the object of Herr von Elterlein's book; and every musical student or amateur can safely trust him as a competent and agreeable guide.

An English translation of this valuable little work is, therefore, most opportune. It will, undoubtedly, assist many a lover of Beethoven's music to appreciate more keenly the beauties of the great master's Sonatas, and will, if possible, enhance his admiration of what may truly be called a book of wisdom.

London, June, 1875.   E. PAUER.

TRANSLATOR'S NOTE.

In preparing a fresh English edition of Herr von Elterlein's book on Beethoven's Pianoforte Sonatas, the translation has been carefully revised with the original, and the author's Prefaces to the first and third German editions have been translated for the first time. The four decades which have elapsed since the book first appeared in Leipzig have added largely to the literature on Beethoven's music which has appeared in Germany. In England, however, the æsthetics of music have been tardy in becoming a branch of literature, and Herr von Elterlein's elucidation of the meaning and character of Beethoven's Sonatas is of a nature which the master's English admirers have not undertaken. Their appreciation of it has been shown by the demand for a further edition of the English translation.

[*July*, 1897.]

AUTHOR'S PREFACE TO THE FIRST EDITION.*

THE following pages claim indulgence as the first attempt—so far as I am aware—at considering Beethoven's Sonatas from an æsthetic point of view. The writer's main object has been to furnish amateurs with a guide and commentary to the study of these the greatest creations in the sphere of pianoforte music. Experienced artists and lovers of art will probably find in the book little that is new. Should it fall to my lot to add hereby a few stones towards the edifice that has yet to be raised—a complete Biography of Beethoven, such as that of Mozart by Ulibischeff—my desire and aim would be more than attained. Ultra Beethovenites may take exception to my criticisms on some of the Sonatas, and to my views on the determining influence of the opus numbering, but it is my intention to state my sentiments candidly,

---

* Of the original.

and to comment on blemishes without reserve. The recourse I have had to various sources of information will not expose me to the accusation of posing in borrowed plumes, for my object in this book has not been my own glorification but to do honour to Beethoven, while to many readers this collecting together of scattered information may prove welcome. My special thanks are due to my friend Rühlmann (State Musician at Dresden) to whom I am indebted for much help and advice and many valuable suggestions. With these words I commend the book to the lovers of Beethoven.

AUTHOR'S PREFACE TO THE THIRD EDITION.*

THIS book now appears in a third edition. It has been partly re-written, and additions have been made. Since its original publication in 1856 the author's views have, in many respects, changed considerably, and his opinions on certain Sonatas have been modified accordingly. During this period the literature about Beethoven has been much increased. First and foremost we have had Marx's Biography—an epoch-making work, though it cannot but be regretted that this great authority on Beethoven should have passed over some works in silence and referred much too briefly to others. What was said in the preface to the first edition about gleaning information from various sources applies no less to the ample use now made of Marx's Biography. Far from this in any way rendering the study of that work superfluous, the present writer would strongly recommend it to

---

* Of the Original.

all who wish to go deeply into the subject. The last part of this volume may perhaps be found a welcome addition by not a few readers. The dates of publication and of probable composition have been taken from Thayer's latest work. In conclusion the author has only to express his grateful thanks for the kind reception given to the former editions by the critics, especially by Dr. Laurencin of Vienna in the "Neue Zeitschrift für Musik"; and also by the music-loving public, as is shown by the demand for a third edition.

August 11th, 1865.

BEETHOVEN'S PIANOFORTE SONATAS.

FIRST PART.

The Sonata in General.

THE Sonata is the greatest and most original production in the province of pianoforte music—its highest exercise and its loftiest aim. Beauty, the ideal of all artistic efforts, may be expressed in the simplest music, but its complete realization can only be attained in the highest forms.

The Sonata may be considered the most perfect form of pianoforte music. The theoretical reasons for this statement are most successfully propounded by Marx, in the third part of his "Compositionslehre." Marx there explains the development of the different forms of pianoforte music in organic order. He begins with the study, proceeds to the fantasia, variation, and rondo, and then to the Sonata, the key-stone and crowning point of all the forms. In another way, Krüger, in his "Beitragen für Leben und Wissenschaft der Tonkunst," arrives at the same result. Like Marx, he establishes a system of musical forms, of which he makes the song form the central point: treating first of the forms that preceded the song form, viz., preludes, toccatos, fantasias; secondly, the song form itself, variations, rondos, fugues: and thirdly, the development of the song form, that is, the union of existing song forms —the Sonata and the Symphony. Krüger considered the three primary forms to be the prelude, song, and Sonata, and that out of these all the others have been developed. The supreme importance of the Sonata form—a form which is also the foundation of the symphony, string quartet, &c.,— is shown by its capability of forming a higher union of the other forms, namely, the song, variation, rondo, and fugue. This was, in fact, indicated by Krüger in the expression, "composition of existing song forms." Indeed, in the Sonata, all these forms recur, and are, so to speak, fused into a concrete and actual unity. According to this view, the Sonata is the organic product of these forms, and this the Beethoven Sonata pre-eminently proves.

If we consider more closely the construction of the Sonata, we shall find it to be divided into several movements—two, three, four, five, or even more—and the plurality of movements may be generally stated as the formal principle of composition. The particular character, however, of the life-picture which a work depicts must always be considered its determining basis. "The soul moulds its own body." ("Die Seele schafft sich ihren Leib.") Musical science must, therefore, in this respect desist from laying down binding laws and immutable principles. Köstlin (in Vischer's "Æsthetik") and Marx (in "Beethoven's Leben und Schaffen") have, ably and exhaustively, propounded and undertaken to prove that the three or four-movement form is the normal principle of construction. Indeed, most Sonatas do contain three or four movements. But, on the other hand, it may be urged that, as will presently be shown, in many of Beethoven's Sonatas, even in some of his most important ones, the two-movement principle strikingly predominates, and to this, from the three and four-movement form, the great master of the Sonata, in the last of these works (Op. cxi.), significantly returns. Marx says, in another place, "That these are only suggestions as to what may have been the determining causes of the form, not fixed conclusions (who can bind the mind?) for it is perfectly clear that the three is as practicable as the four-part form, and that in the future the two and the several movement form will be equally justifiable." This freedom of form appears also in the design and arrangement of the different movements. It will be decided by the character of the entire work, whether, for example, the so-called andante or adagio—generally the slow movement—forms the second or third movement (in the four-movement form), or whether it should stand at the commencement. It is surely unnecessary to specify, that the point in discussion is not the want of form in the composition, but the model on which that form has been framed. Equally indisputable is it that the idea is the only determining principle of the form. This brings us from the form to the matter of the Sonata.

The actual essence of music may be described as the "far dark currents of the soul, the fleeting life, the constant whirl of the world into which all existence and all repose are drawn; as all that rises, hovers, and trembles in the air, and in the heart of man, all that the soul re-echoes to itself from the varied phenomena of movement." (Krüger.) Or we may say, with Carriere (Aesthetik): "It is music which discovers and explains for us the beautiful in the world and in the mind, or still more which shows us, in the movements of the world and of the mind, that inner life which a spiritual nature reveals, so that, amid the external action in which we are engaged, the conditions of mind and soul may express themselves, or through sound make us acquainted with the things of their life. The representation of the ideal in a concrete form is the aim of music, because music is art. The tone-art shows the play of various emotions—it is an ideal representation of the individual life and of its-soul-melodies." As this holds good of music in general, the substance of the Sonata may be briefly described as the subjective life of mind and soul. As Köstlin says, the object of the Sonata is to display a rich, expressive, and subjective state of feeling, whether this flows forth in a rich full stream of emotional images, or whether, in the form of a great tone-picture, one of the different phases of the prevailing sentiment of the emotional life is depicted.

What instrument could be better adapted to such a purpose than the pianoforte? The pianoforte, says Köstlin, since it blends harmony with melody, and yet gives the former into the hands of the subject, is the principal organ for the free, full and safe conduct of the latter; in this instrument the subject is introduced purely for its own sake, and is thus in a position to express itself clearly and completely. The piano is an orchestra in miniature. Marx calls it the ideal instrument.

As is well known, Hanslick has recently* again brought forward his charge of the emptiness of music. He considers it to be only "sounding forms," and compares music with arabesque; but Brendel ("Neue Zeitschrift für musik," vol. 42, No. 8) and Carriere ("Aesthetik," vol. 2, page 322) have thoroughly refuted this opinion. Vischer also, ("Aesthetik," Part 3, page 790) shows the contradiction in which Hanslick involves himself, when he is afterwards obliged to admit that "thought and feeling, the warmest and strongest impulses of the human mind," are the "substance" of music. Brendel aptly says "the feelings of the soul are the substance of music—material which is equally available for all

---

* Written about 1865.   [Translator's Note.]

artists. Now this does not represent mind as having only a vague external connection with technical principles, as a something fleeting and vanishing. Mind and substance are indispensable to music; the succession of sounds is the direct expression of them, the thing itself, and not mere form. Nevertheless, the whole life of music rests on a real psychological basis, and we have no mere combination of sound to deal with."

Let us now turn to the historical realities of the art. Before occupying ourselves exclusively with Beethoven, it is necessary, for many reasons, to give a brief chronological account of the Sonata, from its commencement to its perfection by Beethoven. For the ground-work of this sketch, as far as the time of Haydn, we will make use of the excellent contributions to the history of the Sonata, by J. Faisst, in "Cäcilia," a newspaper now discontinued.

SECOND PART.

The Sonata before Beethoven.

THE earliest beginnings of the Sonata are found towards the close of the seventeenth century. The first Sonatas appeared in 1681, for violin solo by Henry Biber; then in 1683 there appeared twelve Sonatas for violin, violoncello, and piano by the violinist, Corelli. But of more importance as a composer of Sonatas was Johann Kuhnau, Sebastian Bach's predecessor. He first wrote a Sonata in "B" in "New Pianoforte Practice, Part II." ("Neuer Clavierübung anderer Theil.") Taken as a whole, the form is the present one, the Sonata consisting of a quick, a slow, and then a quick movement. The style of writing is polyphonic, but the work fails in inward æsthetic unity. Kuhnau's next work appeared in 1696, under the title of "Fresh Fruit for the Piano;

or, Seven Sonatas for the Pianoforte, excellent in design and style, by Johann Kuhnau." ("Johann Kuhnau, frische Clavierfrüchte, oder sieben Sonaten von guter Invention und Manier auf dem Clavier zu spielen"). These Sonatas show an advance in form and in matter; they are full of energy, vivacity, fresh grace, and also of deep feeling. They contain sometimes four, sometimes five movements, which contrast well with one another in alternations of repose and agitation. The polyphonic treatment is predominant, though the homophonic sometimes breaks through, launching forth into free melodies. Single movements show still greater artistic merit. Kuhnau is intellectually associated with Handel, by his free polyphony and energetic or clear treatment of melody. In some of the movements an inward æsthetic connection is discernible. The next composer to be mentioned in this category is Mattheson. A Sonata appeared by him, in 1713, "dedicated to whoever will play it best," ("derjenigen Person gewidmet, die sie am besten spielen wird.") It consists of one movement only; the treatment of its different parts is richer than with former composers, nor is the theme without merit; but its development shows more external brilliancy than internal wealth.

We come to Domenico Scarlatti. In the first decade of the eighteenth century, he wrote, "30 Sonate per il clavicembalo," and "6 Sonate per il cembalo." Every Sonata contains two parts: the present so-called fantasia (Durchführungstheil) and the third part being blended into one; there is also a similarity to the two-part song-form. The two-part form predominates; the style of writing is more fitted to the instrument than was that of Scarlatti's predecessors; and the crossing of the hands claims notice. With respect to the matter of the Sonatas, Scarlatti himself describes them as "clever tricks of art." They are bright, fresh, lively and intelligent, and often overflow with humour, with touches also of a softer and more earnest feeling; though of a deeper meaning there is no trace.

Scarlatti did not give a new form to the Sonata, in the sense of making it a combination of several movements, but he produced in a style of writing freed from the fetters of polyphony and fitted to the true nature of the instrument, a form regularly matured from the early kernel of the single movement Sonata. This form as the standard, if not for all, at least for the most important movement of the Sonata, and as the most considerable generally among the non-polyphonic forms of an instrumental movement, must have first developed a degree of excellence corresponding to the lofty aim of the Sonata, before what afterwards happened could have been possible, namely, the giving to the Sonata, as a combination of several movements, a systematic and logical shape.

Francesco Durante, the Italian, must be mentioned: he produced an unique work—"Sonate per cembalo divise in studiei divertimenti." In formal construction, these sonatas are a transition between the song-form and the sonata form; they are homophonically written. Considered in the light of historical development, they are deeper than Scarlatti's Sonatas; in a free, natural style of writing, they are a stage beyond Kuhnau; while, as regards matter they may be called valuable and ingenious.

We now approach that musical giant, Sebastian Bach, of whom we will give two examples, the Sonatas in C minor and D minor. The Sonata form—the combination of several movements into one whole re-appears with him. In the Sonatas mentioned he certainly is not, either in form or style, equal in freedom to Scarlatti; he stands nearer to Kuhnau;

but he is far superior to the latter in richness and a free command of means; and on the other hand, he shows himself in advance of Scarlatti, in that he combined several movements into a whole, in accordance with the characteristic style of the Sonata, so that a higher intellectual inner meaning was more apparent than before. Altogether, Bach is the intervening transition step.

The twelve Sonatas by Father Martini, "per l'organo vel cembalo," are another intermediary work. Judging by the character of their composition the Sonatas should have been styled "for the piano," —not "for the organ." In form, they are a medium between the so-called suite and the Sonata proper, being a mixture of polyphony and homophony, and contain plenty of intelligence and life, with very skilful workmanship.

From the middle of the eighteenth century till the death of Emanuel Bach, in 1788, was the beginning of a new period for the Sonata when it acquired a regular form, and one adequate to its conception. Pianoforte literature increased rapidly. Faisst reckons in all 208 Sonatas and 35 composers. After the true, or at least the predominant, form had been found for the single movement of the

Sonata, the object was to give to the Sonata—as a whole formed of several movements—a systematic shape corresponding to its design. These Sonatas, therefore, regularly contain several movements. But this union of several movements into one whole took place in many different ways, and is not so much to be considered as an expression of greater freedom as of indecision, of a striving after a suitable form. The three-movement form predominates, two and four movements are the exception; in the latter, the minuet already appears as the second movement. The form of the single movement is still partly like Scarlatti's, partly more perfect than his was. Movements with a second theme already appear, but the latter is more like a complement to the first theme than a contrast to it; its substance is not so characteristically different, its existence even is often doubtful; hence the weakness of this period. We observe further an enrichment and extension of the song-form, although only an outward one, for its internal expansion leads it into the rondo and sonata-form. Movements with variations, the dance-forms of the minuet and polonaise, and more rarely the rondo-form, already appear. The most prominent name in this period is that of Emanuel Bach, while Johann

Christian Bach, and Leopold Mozart may be briefly mentioned.

The Sonatas of Johann Christian Bach are full of fire, humour, and fresh grace; they resemble to some extent those of Haydn and Mozart. In Leopold Mozart's Sonatas we seem to be already listening to his great son, so much do their style and spirit remind us of the latter.

Emanuel Bach's works display a refined, intelligent, exceedingly intellectual and pleasing nature; we feel with him that everything is the expression of an enthusiastic and noble-minded man. He is Haydn's fore-runner both in the form and matter of his works. The complete and perfect three-movement-form becomes a regular principle of construction with him. His Sonatas contain, as a rule, a first movement, allegro, in the short sonata-form; a second movement, andante, in the song-form; and a third movement, presto, in the rondo-form. His style of writing is generally homophonic. Brendel says of him, in his excellent "History of Music," "Bach by representing, contrary to former composers, the individual mind and feeling of the writer, directly brought in the new instrumental music, and by setting forth individualism in its changing and diverse forms became the founder of modern music." His chief works are his "Sonatas for Connoisseurs and Amateurs." ("Sonaten für Kenner und Liebhaber.")

A new epoch now began : the grandest which the Sonata has ever known, that of Haydn, Mozart, and Beethoven. As in the principal departments of instrumental music, Haydn appears as an epoch-maker, a genius breaking through the old boundaries —in proof of which we have only to refer to his symphonies and quartets—so also did he give to the pianoforte Sonata an important impetus and development, both in form and matter. Although the three-movement-form is mainly to be attributed to Emanuel Bach, the contributions made by Haydn to the progress of the Sonata were: that he repeated the principal theme of the first part of a movement in the third part, that he regularly settled the second, so-called fantasia part, and the third, so-called repetition part, into the Sonata form ; that he reduced what had before been the mere humour and caprice of the composer, and in many of the earlier works had not even been found at all, into an unchanging principle of construction ; that by these means he raised, enriched and amplified the single movement—which means the Sonata generally—that he reached a higher unity, and created a stronger and more uniform whole. There necessarily followed the development of the substance of the Sonata. The chief thought gained importance by repetition; more especially as Haydn had given to it a decided and characteristic expression, which he firmly maintained throughout the movement. Indeed the principal movements of the Haydn Sonata have an uniform fundamental thought firmly and decidedly stamped on them. Not only does the single movement show this unity, but the collective movements of the Sonata form a much more uniform whole, proceed more from a settled basis, and are much more closely connected together than in the works of previous writers. I say "much more," for the unity that we find in Beethoven, a unity that was absolute, because it rested on a psychological basis, is not yet apparent; we have rather, if I may use the expression, the stringing together of several movements united by one common sentiment. But what is the ruling sentiment? It is that spirit of naïve and child-like cheerfulness, that teasing play of jest and mirth, that roguish humour, that caprice and frolicksomeness; in short, all

Haydn's music reflects the thoughts and feelings of his artistic nature. Köstlin well says that Haydn brought in the epoch of free style, the golden age and spring-time of the musical art, that with him music becomes conscious that she is not a mere system and science, but a free impulse and a lyric poem. Brendel calls Haydn the greatest master of jest and humour. However limited Haydn's world may be, compared to the boundless vistas which Beethoven has revealed to us, however little Haydn's child-like nature may show us of the deep secrets of the soul, yet he is in his own sphere so inventive, so rich in genius, that a place belongs to him among the first of the tone artists; and he who has thoroughly entered into the gigantic conceptions of Beethoven may still turn back, now and then, to a Sonata of "Father Haydn," to enjoy, as it were, a picture of his own past childhood, and to pass once again through the first paradise of life. Among Haydn's numerous Sonatas, two only need here be specified: the one in E flat major, and a smaller one in B minor.

Mozart was Haydn's real successor in the department of the Sonata. He gave it a further development in many directions. Mozart adhered also to the principle, received from Haydn, of starting with a definite and expressive theme, and making it the basis of the movement. But this did not satisfy him : he wanted a something by which a greater diversity, together with a more intellectual unity, should be attained, and this something was the cantabile, or the second subject, which Mozart introduced into the first movement of the Sonata. He composed longer and richer phrases of melody, larger and broader periods, established a more defined difference between light and shade, divided both into larger divisions of time, and precise periods, and thus produced a definite distinction between the tender and the vigorous parts, a greater clearness and decision in the form and in the sequence of thought. Another characteristic feature of his Sonatas, is the perfect beauty of form, which, in system, symmetry and regularity, shows itself alike in small and great. This is the natural result of a perfect and harmonious nature. As Brendel and others have well shown Mozart's artistic individuality revealed, from the very beginning and throughout, the purest harmony of mind and soul, a quiet self-contained balance of powers, a condition of the inner life in which the moral struggles are hushed, or at most form but the far dark back-ground. This primary adjustment imparted that gracefulness of thought, which is another characteristic feature of his music. This is such an essential quality with him, that when he depicts violent passion, he holds himself far aloof from roughness; everything is so closely enfolded in a beautiful garb, that the passion is, so to speak, stifled. It is only Mozart, the artist, who struggles; Mozart, the man, came out conqueror long ago. In this respect, Mozart's Symphony and Quintet in G minor are especially characteristic. As regards the Sonatas, it must be frankly admitted that Mozart stands far higher in other departments of instrumental music. The most important Sonata is unquestionably the C minor with the fantasia before it; beside this rank the F major, A minor, the Sonata for two performers in F major, and a few others. On the foundation laid by the Haydn and Mozart Sonata, Beethoven reared his gigantic edifice, to the consideration of which we now turn.*

---

* From this historical sketch Clementi may with propriety be omitted, for his *forte* was the *technique* of pianoforte playing, in which even Beethoven scarcely excelled him.

THIRD PART.

Beethoven.

AS Beethoven, in his instrumental music generally, took his starting point from Haydn and Mozart, so in his Sonatas he first trod in the footsteps of these composers. But when he had reached greater maturity and independence, Beethoven left these paths, struck out a new way and took a fresh aim. He improved both the form and matter of the Sonata, breathed into it a spirit, such as Haydn and Mozart had never known; in a word, gave to it that peculiar, and as yet unreached, depth and grandeur, which ever awaken afresh the unqualified admiration of the true lover of music. Unlike Haydn and Mozart, Beethoven became so absorbed in this species of composition, and displayed in it so much of the essential character of his genius, that Hand, in his "Aesthetics of Musical Art," comes to the conclusion that Beethoven's originality is pre-eminently displayed in his Sonatas. This is overstating the case, for Beethoven is at his greatest in the symphonies and quartets, though it it is true that the Sonatas give us one of the best opportunities for fully understanding him. It is in these pre-eminently that the stages of Beethoven's artistic development may be traced with the greatest certainty, for even Beethoven was not all at once what he became in his prime. The gradual growth and ripening of his mind—surely one of the most interesting psychological periods in the course of a great artist's evolution—is more clearly illustrated in his sonatas than in his other works. Nowhere else are those fine gradual changes, that progress towards an ever increasing independence, so noticeable and so traceable. For what an unbridged chasm exists between the second and third symphonies, between the Quartets, op. 18, and those three constellations, op. 59. The Sonatas surrounding and connecting these works form the intermediary stages, build the bridge over the chasm, and solve the problem. If the question be now asked: What are the contents of the Beethoven sonatas? the answer will be found in the following analyses of each separate work. Meanwhile we must set forth some leading considerations and the general point of view from which the examination of details must proceed; in other words we must depict the nature of Beethoven's artistic individuality and the general features of his instrumental music in order to get a sound basis for the apprehension of the particular and the special.

The essential characteristic of his genius is, in my opinion, wealth of imagination, united with a nature full of foreboding and unfathomable depths,* but irradiated by a lofty intellect, and sustained by strong moral determination.† In Beethoven, imagination, feeling, intellect and character are developed with equal potency and import, and in perfect harmony with each other. It is to these fundamentals that the finest works are unmistakably to be traced, indeed, they seem to me to be their inevitable outcome. Nor can this close connection

---

* Kullak says, in his excellent work on " The Beautiful in Music ": " No one has ever felt more devoutly than Bach, more happily than Mozart, or with more gigantic power than Beethoven."

† Richard Wagner says ("Kunstwerk der Zukunft ") with regard to the C minor symphony, " Beethoven raised the expression of his music almost to a moral determination."

of fancy, feeling, intellect and character be realised except by a strong subjectiveness, not one-sided or wrapt up in itself, but in unison with objective qualities equally potent.

In contrast to Mozart and other composers, Beethoven has been called a pre-emintly subjective artist, with whom form was subservient to subjective contents. There is some truth in this assertion, but we must guard against misunderstanding, for, with all his self-absorption, Beethoven had more true objectiveness than many of the soi-disant objective composers. Such fully developed, tensely strung subjectiveness can rarely exist without a struggle, at least not without violent agitation and emotion could it come into being, and into contact with other existences. Do we not find this to be the case with Beethoven? Köstlin says, that with Beethoven music, being a reflection of himself and his relation to the objective world, is alike the attraction and repulsion of the subjective through the objective into the innermost and all pervading ego. All these peculiarities appear prominently in Beethoven's instrumental music; and it has long been recognized that his forte lies in this, and not in vocal music.

Concerning the idiosyncrasy of Beethoven's instrumental music, Brendel, with admirable conciseness, writes thus, in his "Musical History:" "The chief characteristic of Beethoven's instrumental music is the increased power of the subject-matter, which results in the heightening and extending of all the means of expression. Following this increased significance of the matter, we see a striving after the utmost clearness of expression, by which music alone, not united to words, is made capable of representing definite states of mind. In earlier times, with Haydn and Mozart, the common character of instrumental music was a free play of vague, general expression. Beethoven, on the contrary, expressed definite situations, and pourtrayed clearly recognizable states of mind. Closely allied with this was his endeavour to set a poetical image before the mind of the hearer, while the dramatic life of his compositions was evolved by development of the matter. Mozart's aim had been an intelligent and logical working out of the form which a piece of music took. But with Beethoven the formal treatment ceases to be a leading consideration, and the tone-poet, following his poetical object, brings before us a grand soul-picture, pourtraying every variety of emotion. Finally, the humorous element also plays its part in his works."

Beethoven's Sonatas, reflecting as they do the artistic personality of their composer, are distinguished by the increased importance of their contents, the representation of definite states of mind, and their poetic tendency. The range is indeed in no way so comprehensive as, for example, it is in the symphony. In the latter the sentiment is preponderatingly objective and general in character, pervaded though by a Beethoven subjectiveness. In the Sonatas Beethoven refers only to his innermost self. Buried in the secrets of his own heart, to the piano alone does he confide the concerns of his inmost soul. These works we will now review; but before doing so we must say a few words on the style and periods of Beethoven's creations. It has been already intimated that at first Beethoven trod in the paths of his predecessors, Haydn and Mozart; yet in the works belonging to that time his individuality continually becomes more conspicuous. This is the first period. Then Beethoven has emancipated himself, stands alone, has reached maturity and independence, has become a man in the fullest sense of the word. This is the second period. In the course of his artistic life, partly in consequence of outward, partly of inward circumstances, Beethoven continually retreats into himself; he, so to speak, isolates his soul's life, raises his subjectiveness to a point at which the artist appears an isolated being, and only the most individual feelings are represented. This is called the third period. To the first period the first twenty or thirty works are, on an average, assigned; to the second, those up to a hundred; and to the third period, the works beyond that number. To draw a definite boundary line is in the nature of things impossible; since at the time of publication, as now the numbers prefixed to the works did not, in a great measure, at all correspond to the time of their composition; therefore, the so-called opus numbers can afford no criterion. Then, again, everything in Beethoven's works flows in such a living stream that abstract divisions cannot be set up between single works; the transitions are too fine. Marx, in his excellent book on Beethoven, goes too far when he rejects these periods as lifeless limitations. In its essence, indeed, Beethoven's style certainly is but one and the same; that something which distinguishes him from other masters is apparent from the very beginning. Yet such characteristic differences arise in this unity, that each period surely has its raison d'être.

FOURTH PART.

Beethoven's Sonatas.

BEETHOVEN'S Sonatas may be divided into groups; but deferring this for the present, we will, without further preface, closely examine them according to their opus numbers, and reserve other considerations for the last part.

OP. 2, No. 1, F MINOR.

Appeared in 1796. *Dedicated to Joseph Haydn.*

This Sonata is distinguished throughout by the consistent development of a fundamental thought, by which, with much diversity of detail, an uniform character is given to the whole, or, as Marx puts it, a series of moods and feelings is psychologically developed as a subjective whole.

A certain discontentedness runs through the first

movement, allegro, F minor, 4-4 time; a mild restlessness, a half shy seeking for something and not finding it. This we see if we do but look at the characteristic form of the first and second subjects, and at the opposite treatment which each receives. (Compare Marx, "Beethoven," vol. I, p. 122). What then remains but quietly to submit? Does not the third subject, shortly before the close of the first part, and also before the end of the whole movement, the passage marked con expressione, suggest this? There is all through the movement a breath of really passionate yearning, but only a breath; it does not come to a real struggle, and to sharp contrasts; the piece has a sort of bittersweetness about it.

Marx calls the second movement, adagio, F major, 3-4 time, a child's prayer. "It comforts if it does not find a hearing, yet the anxiety depicted in the first movement has not disappeared, but in the tributary subject quietly, though unobtrusively, makes itself felt." Perfect peace breathes through these strains; it is only in passing that anything painful arises to darken the picture; and then the cloudlet soon disappears, and it is clear sunshine again. Few of Beethoven's movements bear such an impress of placidity. This gentleness is also to some extent expressed in the other movements.

The repose of the adagio was but passing. In the third movement, menuetto allegretto, F minor, $\frac{3}{4}$ time, the mind of the tone-poet falls back into the discontent and restless yearning of the first movement. "No rest and no peace" (keine Rast und keine Ruh,) is the impression produced by the minuet and by the trio in F major, and the climax of this sentiment in the second part of the minuet is very fine.

But now, in the fourth movement, prestissimo, F minor, $\frac{4}{4}$ time, a storm rises in the soul; as Marx finely says, when fortune fails we behold the courage of suffering and the indignation of a noble mind, struggling with unworthy troubles, and if not crowned with conquest, possessed of the victory. In this movement, the dominant and basic sentiment rises to real passion, which is effectively expressed by the sweeping trills and the well-marked chief theme. Only for a moment in the first part is a quieter sentiment perceptible; then, at the beginning of the second part a soothing melody predominates for a time, and the expression becomes deeply fervent. But this image of bliss gradually disappears, for the waves of passion sweep onward again, ever stronger and more irrepressible, the storm and rushing begin afresh and retain the mastery until the end. The finale is indisputably the finest movement of the Sonata; it is beautifully finished, and the distribution of light and shade is excellent. Lenz, in "Beethoven et ses Trois Styles," says of it, "Un morceau si franc si dramatique, qu'il n'en existait pas dans le temps qui pût lui être comparé." The radical principle of the Sonata is decidedly Mozartish, whether as regards the form or the matter, especially the principal subject though there is no doubt that in the finale, both as a whole and in detail, the later Beethoven already appears; the elevation and energy of the last movement, and the transition from the second to the third part of it exhibit the true Beethoven.

OP. 2, No. 2, A MAJOR.

Appeared in 1796. Dedicated to Joseph Haydn.

This Sonata is distinguished by an almost equally uniform and consecutive, if not quite so compact and clear a development of the primary thought, as the preceding work, to which, it is throughout inferior in elevation of style, while to a certain extent superior in originality. In the first movement, allegro vivace, ¾ time, Beethoven at once strikes quite a new chord. How courageously and self-reliantly the first theme is announced, how boldly and cleverly it is carried out, how striking are the scales and modulations! A youthful and even wanton humour is the leading idea. Marx sees in fancy, a restless boy who does not know how to give vent to his overflowing vitality. However, a deep, yearning feeling arises, just as if this wanton play of humour could not possibly ensure true and lasting satisfaction. This is the tributary subject in E minor, which appears in A minor in the second part. The whole movement is cast in one mould, and is full of a fresh and uniformly harmonious expression of feeling. Already, the original genius of Beethoven distinctly appears, and the first dawnings of the later Beethoven humour are perceptible. The movement contains passages—such as the one which, at the entrance of the second part, is first worked up in C, and then comes to rest in the same key, the passage further on in E major, just before the return of the first subject, and others also—which contain nothing akin to Mozart.

In the second movement, largo appassionato, D

major, ¾ time, feeling, humour and fancy make way for a more exalted sentiment. There is something sublime in the procession of those quiet, measured melodies and harmonies. Lenz remarks that the style of the piece reminds one of Handel. Profound but restrained agitation pervades the movement. Very impressive is the entrance of the D minor in the second half of the piece, the diversion into B major, and then the return into D major with the repetition of the first subject in a higher octave; by this, and by the conclusion which immediately follows, a quiet touch of glory is added to the picture, and the whole is rounded off in beauty. Marx well says: "The song is quiet and solemn, like the thoughts of a noble mind alone under the starry firmament;" and the entrance of the minor, he adds, produces a thrilling emotion as if words like death and eternity had fallen on the heart.

The scherzo allegretto, A major, ¾ time, which follows as the third movement is a lively, bright composition, "charmingly alluring," reminiscent, as is also the minor (trio), of the Haydn-Mozart minuet form, and in no way attaining to the originality of the first two movements. Lenz finds in the trio the character of Russian and Sclavonic melodies.

The fourth movement, rondo grazioso, A major, $\frac{2}{4}$ time, is a picture of easy, cheerful life; with no touch of the Beethoven of the first movement; this movement, the chief theme especially, is decidedly Mozartish in conception; there is an agreeable play of sounds, but a deeper meaning is wanting. The formal musical structure is, however, interesting; the rondo-form being originally treated. On this point I would refer the reader to the third part of Marx's "Compositionslehre," in which he speaks of the movement as the best specimen of the Rondo-form Beethoven has given us. The Sonata, as a whole, consists of two unequal parts; the last two movements not fully corresponding in style and expression to the two first. Marx also thinks that the psychological unity of the last movement is not in harmony with the first movements.

OP. 2, No. 3, C MAJOR.

Appeared in 1796. Dedicated to Joseph Haydn.

This Sonata, also, though resting as a whole on Mozart's principles, reveals the later Beethoven in particular passages, and, with the exception, perhaps, of the second movement, it has a steadily developed uniform idea lying at its basis. A bright, active life, full of youthful freshness and vigour, pervades the first movement, allegro con brio, C major, $\frac{4}{4}$ time, Nor is gracefulness wanting, as the passages marked dolce, in G major, and E major, respectively, in the first and second parts, abundantly prove. On the other hand, the picture is not without its humorous side (see motive at bar 19, before the conclusion of the first part). Storm and hurry are well depicted by the rolling up and down of the octaves. The so-called fantasia part contains some very fine writing, and shows more freedom than in the works of earlier composers, but the most original part seems to me to be the point d'orgue on the chord of A flat major, followed by an interesting cadence, leading back to the first theme, and ending in a powerful and magnificent conclusion. In the whole of the Coda, Beethoven boldly discards the strict sonata-form for the free form of the fantasia.

A deep devoutness pervades the first theme of the second movement, adagio, E major, $\frac{3}{4}$ time; a sense of inward contentment and happiness breathes through its tones. Soon, however, with the appearance of the E minor, a yearning impulse, not without pain and sorrow, is manifested. (Entrance of the A and B minor in fortissimo). Further on, the first theme returns soothingly, and in C major fortissimo it even rises to an expression of courageous confidence. It is true that the yearning begins again, but it is materially subdued, the pain is dulled, and the first theme is heard for the last time, an octave higher—sounding as it were from a glorified height—and, in a calm, beatified mood the movement ends. The colouring, the shading, the modulation, are all fresh, new, original, sometimes even magical; we have true tone-poetry, soul painting, such as was peculiar to Beethoven alone.

After this movement what can the third movement —the allegro scherzo, C major, $\frac{3}{4}$ time—mean? Its character is careless, self-satisfied cheerfulness; the form is still that of the Haydn-Mozart minuet, the Beethoven scherzo has not appeared. The trio in A minor is not without originality, with its almost wilful sequence of the upper and lower registers; the former restless, fleeting, surging, in contrast to the hopefulness of the latter. The tone colouring of the whole is original, and an excellent preparation for the character of the finale.

This fourth movement, allegro assai, C major, $\frac{6}{8}$ time, is full of the most sparkling life, a little Bacchanalia, the product of bold, youthful petulance, an episode in a period of "Sturm und Drang." The motive in F major (dolce) in the middle of the movement forms an agreeable contrast, and serves to enhance the sparkle and dash of the whole. This movement reaches its climax in the shake towards the end; the shake here becomes the most direct and the most striking expression of the Bacchanalian whirl. The A major, which follows without intermission, has a striking effect, and like the powerful conclusion, which immediately ensues, is a true Beethoven trait. Particular passages remind us, now and then of Mozart, but the whole is, as it were, cast in one mould by some new being, and it seems sometimes, with its Bacchanalian revelry, to foreshadow, though as yet quite faintly, the A major Symphony. Lenz says that the movement is a sort of rondo à la chasse, and he perceives the "Halali" quite distinctly. Let him have that as he will; the law of working up the sentiment to a climax is fulfilled in this Sonata by this finale. But, I ask again, what has the second movement to do with the organism of the whole? An inner connection between it and the other movements is wanting; it belongs to a later stage of development. Lenz seems also to be of this opinion. He somewhat fancifully says that one lingers before the piece as before the Venus of Milo in the Louvre; and adds, one would do well to play the movement apart from the whole Sonata.

OP. 6, D MAJOR.

Appeared in the winter, of 1796-7. *Date of composition uncertain.*

This is the only Sonata for two performers on the pianoforte which Beethoven has written. It is in the small sonata-form, and is certainly a work of Beethoven's earliest youth, a work which can in no way be compared to the preceding Sonatas, and which is far surpassed even by Mozart's charming little pianoforte duet Sonatas. There is nothing more to say about the work. It is decidedly doubtful whether Beethoven had anything to do with its publication, as op. 6; it is far more likely that this was the work of some uncalled for hand.

OP. 7, E FLAT MAJOR.

Appeared in 1797. *Dedicated to the Countess Babette von Keglevics.*

As regards the first two movements this Sonata is an important one. The first movement, allegro molto con brio, E flat major $_8^6$ time, is a tone-picture rich in colour and character. The aroma of the later romantic feeling is shed over its tone-images; one has the impression of going into a garden, gorgeous with a profusion of the finest and brightest flowers, most skilfully arranged—so splendidly do the tone-pictures group themselves and enhance each other's glory. At the same time, this many coloured play of sounds is full of soul; that shadow may not be wanting to the light, a few earnest touches are interspersed here and there, the humorous strains not being forgotten. This will suffice to indicate the richness of the picture; the reverent player and hearer will easily understand everything, and the rare beauties of the music will speedily reveal themselves.

The second movement, largo con gran expressione, E major, ¾ time, strikes a higher note. The substance of the movement may be described in a single word, deep-thoughtfulness (Tiefsinn). A sacred and exalted tone pervades these strains, which give an insight into the depths of the soul. The master seems to have been caught up into higher spheres than those in which he had just lingered. I only say he seems to have been caught up, for he soon feels that a yet higher world lies before him, and a strong yearning after it moves his soul (see the motive in A flat major, bar 25). Stronger and stronger becomes the pressure; blows resound that shatter heart and marrow; it is as if fate were knocking at the door, and the soul were reminded of the pain of living by the rough reality of existence. What a powerful, dramatic passage! The yearning becomes less ardent, and touching plaintive tones fall on the ear, the soul calms itself into quiet resignation, and with the return of the first theme sinks into its former deep reflection and reverent meditation. Once again is the tone-poet seized with a painful longing after those lighter spheres; but the feeling of what he has been soaring after, of what, in spite of all things, he has won, now takes permanent possession of him, and he rises into a happy trance. In this mode the movement closes. We find in it what is as yet the most melancholy of adagii, for in it real soul-secrets are unveiled; we have the tone-poet Beethoven again with us. In the following movements, Beethoven, alas, descends from the height to which he had attained.

The third movement, allegro, E flat major, ¾ time, and minore, E flat minor, certainly is, as regards the latter, with its persistent restless trills, its harmony and modulations, of a highly original stamp, "a fanciful and plaintive melody, like that of an old German ballad" (Ulibischeff), inclining itself, as Marx says, to an inward unquiet rumination and brooding, being in no way an unworthy successor to the first two movements; but the allegro, and especially the fourth movement, rondo allegretto, E flat major, $\frac{2}{4}$ time, are, as regards substance and form, of a strikingly Haydn-Mozartish character, without any prominent originality. They merely present a vague, general play of sounds, and the finale is over-loaded with uninteresting figures and passages. The defect of the Sonata throughout is a want of climax: it shows what a strong hold Beethoven's predecessors still had over him. He has only attained a temporary triumph as yet.

OP. 10, No. 1, C MINOR.

Appeared in 1798. Dedicated to the Countess von Browne.

In the sequence of the movements this Sonata is characterised by one very steadily developed fundamental thought; it is, however, with the exception, perhaps, of the last movement, written in the Mozart manner. The first movement, allegro molto, C minor, $\frac{3}{4}$ time, seems as if the composer had been over-hearing his great fore-runner, to whom one might unhesitatingly ascribe the movement, so entirely in Mozart's spirit are the chief themes and their working out. Everything recalls Mozart's great C minor Sonata. The underlying thought of the movement may be called subdued, restrained passion.

Through the second movment, adagio molto, A flat major, $\frac{2}{4}$ time, there breathes that Mozartish spirit (Innigkeit) which was not the result of a mental struggle, and which has no such dark background, but emanates from a mind at rest with itself. In correspondence with this is the whole style of the composition, which, without any very special originality in melody, harmony, and modulation, is a reproduction of Mozart, though, of course, not a slavish but an intelligent one. The difference between Beethoven and Mozart will be fully appreciated by comparing this movement with the Largo of the previous Sonata, or by playing the two immediately after each other. The conclusion of the movement is very well-devised.

The third movement of the Sonata, prestissimo, C minor $\frac{4}{4}$ time, is, on the other hand, the most original. The two chief subjects and their development are quite unique; something of the true

Beethoven spirit pervades the whole. The master departs from his model and seeks his own paths. There is no more reticence or restraint, lively emotion fills the heart, a small battle almost begins; The agitation, however, is not profound. It seems as if the aim of the struggle were to shake off the melancholy character of the minor, the C major continually breaks through, and is in the end triumphant. One might say "that's the humour of it."

OP. 10, No. 2, F MAJOR.

Appeared in 1798. *Dedicated to the Countess von Browne.*

In the first and last movements of this sonata Beethoven is under the influence of Haydn. The jocose, cheerful, easy nature of the merry, roguish Haydn runs through the first movement, allegro, F major $\frac{2}{4}$ time. The first subject is a striking instance of this. It is a delightful ensemble, full of diverse changes, and of surprises, such as the entrance of the D major, while certain passages bear decided marks of originality. But this is all that can be said for the movement; even the enthusiastic Lenz calls it meagre.

The second movement, however, allegro, F minor, $\frac{3}{4}$ time transports us into Beethoven's world. Here are the germs of the Beethoven scherzo ; the master stretches out far beyond the forms of the Haydn-Mozart minuet, and produces a most original creation. The whole is so imaginative, so ætherial, and has such a magical effect, that it awakens in me a feeling like that of Goethe's words, in "Faust."

> "Wolkenzug und Nebelflor
> Erhellen sich von oben,
> Luft im Laub und Wind im Rohr
> Und Alles ist zerstoben."

Lenz says that it brings before us a Brocken-mountain scene from "Faust," while Marx calls attention to the reposeful harmonies in D flat major, in the middle movements and justly asks, "Is it, then, only in melody, only in movement, that poetry is to be found?"

In the third movement, prestissimo, F major, $\frac{2}{4}$ time, Beethoven relapses into the style of Haydn. It is constructed on one motive, and pervaded by a Puckish spirit ; as Marx observes, a mischievous game between Fugue and Sonata is carried on ; the former seeming to resemble an old man with a child pulling his beard. To this apt observation we have nothing to add but that it is useless to seek in this movement for a trace of the Beethoven, whose idiosyncracy has already frequently been revealed.

OP. 10, No. 3, D MAJOR.

Appeared in 1798.   *Dedicated to the Countess von Browne.*

In this, which Marx calls the first great Sonata, we clearly recognize the later Beethoven, especially in the first two movements. What storm and dash there is in the first movement, presto, D major, $\frac{4}{4}$ time! How characteristic is the ascent of the first notes in unison from the bass note D to A the fifth above, and then the broken octaves to the tenth above, F sharp, which by the combination of an opposite descending passage to the A, below the staff are rendered still more expressive. The resistless rushing and hurrying, the "Sturm und Drang," depicted in the opening passage are repeated and intensified, till there is scarcely a moment of rest; the reposeful motive in A major, in the first part, is powerless to still the raging of the storm. The whole movement is extremely rich in passages of special beauty. Particularly noticeable is the masterly power with which the motive of the first four notes, D, C sharp, B, A, is worked out, the numerous and characteristic forms in which it appears, and still more remarkable is the iron energy displayed in the fantasia part, and at bar 38, before the conclusion of the first part, in the proudly pacing bass notes and stormily descending octaves, interwoven with which is the humorous motive at bar 32—a passage which re-appears in the third part. This movement is not only full of lyric power, but is in the highest degree dramatic; it is pervaded by youthful vigour and heroism; and in fancy, we can see, though only as yet in the dim distance, the creator of the "Eroica" symphony.

The second movement, largo, D minor, $\frac{6}{8}$ time, is a worthy associate of the first. Marx aptly characterizes its meaning as one of dismal fretting and depressing melancholy. It bespeaks deep, manly sorrow born with fortitude; in the A major motive the mind finds temporary rest, only to be speedily overwhelmed with a deep impassioned sorrow, which slowly subsides, and gently dies away. And now for the musical representation of such a subject! Does it remind us of Beethoven's predecessors? Not in the least. Here, as in fact, in the first movement, the greatness of the later Beethoven is already apparent, so new and original is the composition. And again the dramatic feeling makes itself felt, especially where the chief subject is heard in the low bass, with a restless, stormy accompaniment, first in demi-semi-quavers, then in semi-demi-semi-quavers in the treble—a powerful and striking passage! And how well does the thrice-repeated G sharp, shortly before the close, depict the keen, cutting inward woe! This largo surpasses any of the slow movements hitherto mentioned, and also many of those in the later Sonatas. Unfortunately, the other parts of the Sonata are not up to the level of the first two movements.

The third movement, minuetto, D major, ¾ time, sunnily bright as both it and the teasing G major trio are, does not accord well with the unfathomable depths of sorrow of the largo. Marx, however, thinks differently, and considers the movement as a correct and necessary member in the organism of the piece. (Compare his "Compositionslehre," part 3). Supposing that in the inward, as in the outward world, there is a refreshing sunshine clearing up all the mysteries of darkness, and granting that psychological correctness requires that brightness and light should follow the night which had gathered round the largo, still it seems to me that the movement in question has too much of that light Haydnish cheerfulness, I might say too little of the ideality of form which was peculiar to Beethoven, when in good spirits and quite himself, to be considered as in clear and necessary connection with the previous movements. I always have the impression that Beethoven lost his cue here; I miss the working up of the ruling thought.

Nor does the fourth movement, rondo allegro, D major, $\frac{2}{4}$ time, supply this want. It certainly is more characteristic than the third movement; the first motive is original and worked out into the most diverse forms, in a masterly manner, while the whole is exceedingly lively and not without humour. But the influence of Beethoven's predecessors, which in the largo, was slightly perceptible, and in the first movement scarcely seen at all, is apparent at intervals. After the depth and grandeur of the first two movements, the tone and keeping of the whole of this movement appears to me too light and fleeting, and the humour too shallow, to give an impression of any striking internal unity, or to form an adequate conclusion to the whole work.

OP. 13, C MINOR.

Appeared 1799. *Dedicated to Prince Lichnowsky.*

In this Sonata Beethoven again attains a very

close unity between the movements. The work has always enjoyed a special preference among dilettanti. It may be described as one of the master's most popular compositions, and is the ne plus ultra with those who have not arrived at an understanding of the later works, such as Op. 57. The name "Pathétique" may have contributed to this, as has also the fact that the Sonata is easy to play, more easy to play than, for example, the last named composition. But the intellectual contents of the work, the plastic soul-pictures, explain the preference; the Sonata comes very near to the emotional understanding, and the title "Pathétique" is striking and not easily mistaken, although other works are equally, if not more, pathetic. Here the pathos is deep, earnest passion, which, however, does not overstep a certain measure of gravity, and dignified deportment. The first movement, grave, then allegro molto con brio, C minor, $\frac{4}{4}$ time is the most telling expression of this primary character, a life-like picture of manly, earnest, painful and passionate emotion. In the stately introduction the ardour seems restrained; here and there the fire breaks out, in a marked rhythm, but only to be immediately quenched. But at the entrance of the allegro, the lava stream bursts its bounds, and rushes forth. In the tributary subject, in E flat minor, and then more intensely in D flat major, a pleading, soothing voice is heard restraining the storm. But in vain is the stream arrested. A moment's pause is perceptible in the passage marked grave; then the storm begins anew and with increased vehemence in E minor. And again arise those beseeching, soothing strains in F minor and C minor. But in vain; the storm must spend itself, till at length it subsides in a diminished chord of the seventh. A third time the grave appears, and then a last short outburst, followed by deep repose. Marx points out the repeated appearance of the grave as particularly significant. Says he: "It does not stand there as an empty clang of sounds or chords, but has its own specific purpose in the mind of the composer, and is in accordance with the character and intention of the whole; three times before the end it portentously points back to the solemn introduction to the work." The nature of this grave gives the impression that it could be the product only of some strong determination.

The sharp struggle being over, in the second movement, Adagio cantabile, A flat major, $\frac{3}{4}$ time, a profound peace takes possession of the master's soul, and is well expressed in the sustained singing theme. The feeling becomes more and more deep and reverent, and rises, in the end, to real rapture. Once only, when the theme is heard in A flat minor, a cry of sorrow escapes; but this produces courageous, joyful exaltation (transition to E major); a moment, and the untroubled forms of rest and peace again hover around us.

The third movement, rondo allegro, C minor, $\frac{3}{4}$ time, gives completeness to the whole. The storm which swept through the soul in the first movement has subsided, the tone-poet has saved and ensured his inward peace; his mind has, in a measure, purified itself.

The finale seems the outcome of this purifying process—its most direct expression. More strictly speaking, the result is a certain submission to something that was inevitable, but a happy, courageous submission, full of power for fresh exertions, and renewed activity. There runs also through this movement an active, though not unquiet life-current in many changing forms, "bewegt und doch massvol Alles,"—a satisfactory conclusion. It is not to be denied that the last movement, both in its chief subject and in other particulars of its formal construction, reminds one very much of Mozart, far more so than does the finale of the previous Sonata.

OP. 14, Nos. 1 and 2, E MAJOR and G MAJOR.

Appeared 1799 ; when composed, uncertain. Dedicated to the Baroness Braun

After the D major Sonata, Op. 6, these Sonatas are the weakest of the works hitherto under consideration and are very inferior to Op. 2.

The whole of the second Sonata might be unhesitatingly ascribed to Haydn, while the first is a little more independent, but so little that, although it would do honour to the pupil, it does none to the master. Through Schindler, these Sonatas have received what one might almost call an undeserved celebrity ; at any rate, one which Beethoven did not anticipate. Schindler makes mention in his Biography of Beethoven, of a conversation with him in the year 1823, in which Beethoven describes the contents of the Sonata as a dialogue between man and wife, or between lover and mistress, as the conflict of two principles. Marx in his work on Beethoven, takes much trouble to place the purport and import of this remark in a right light ; that is, to reduce it to proper proportions. We quite agree with him that Beethoven's words contained no special reference to the works in question. Indeed, all instrumental music presents contrasts, like the image of the man and woman; conflicting principles, such as are frequently found in Haydn and Mozart: in an æsthetic point of view, therefore, the observation proves nothing or too much, for Beethoven has, in other works, composed more clever dialogues. Supposing that these Sonatas do represent a conversation between a man and a woman, it does not add to their importance; but Marx demonstrates that they do not display the least trace of dialogue. Like Marx we may find these Sonatas attractive and very charming, but for Beethoven we seek in vain. Their meaning is so obvious, the feelings which they depict are so simple and direct that any further explanation would be superfluous.

OP. 22, B FLAT MAJOR.

Composed, 1800. Dedicated to the Count von Browne.

In the first two movements of this Sonata deeper chords are again struck. The first movement, allegro con brio, B flat major $\frac{4}{4}$ time is distinguished by energy and strong youthful vitality; a fresh pulse of life beats through these tones, a joyful, courageous feeling pervades the whole. Very characteristic is the first theme; it gives the signal for brisk action, which is depicted in brilliant passages ranging through both registers, and is interrupted only by the firm courageous entry of the second subject in thirds and sixths. Towards the end of the first part there is a third motive in octaves, majestically rising and falling, and suggesting the appearance of an earnest, manly form in the midst of a gay youthful crowd. The second part introduces a new and characteristic feature. It appears, at first, like some strange apparition whose entrance causes a precipitate retreat among the surrounding elements; but the scattered forms gradually re-unite, the treble performing passages of rapidly-rolling semi-quavers, while the bass moves to and fro in crotchets and quavers; after which comes a momentary pause. In the third part, with the return of the chief theme, the former chequered movement recommences, as if the composer wished to be serious once more before he concluded, although only for an instant. In some parts of the movement we are still reminded of Mozart, but, in general, Beethoven's originality decidedly appears.

As much cannot be said for the second movement, adagio, E flat major, $\frac{6}{8}$ time. A deep yearning breathes through the first theme, a pleasant calm and atmosphere of romance pervade the entire movement; but, at the same time, the whole seems somewhat weak; it might be said that the melody was tinged with the lusciousness of the best kind of Italian music, and was thus foreign to the Beethoven of our imagination. Although this movement is no improvement on the first, it is not inferior to it, as the last two movements unfortunately are. In point of fact—and Lenz agrees in this—Beethoven decidedly relapses into the Haydn-Mozart style of writing, both in the third movement, minuet, B flat major, $\frac{3}{4}$ time, and also in the fourth, rondo allegretto, B flat major, $\frac{2}{4}$ time. A cheerful, ordinary, tone of feeling, wanting in individual expression, characterises both these movements; and they have but little originality.

OP. 26, A FLAT MAJOR.

Composed, 1801.   *Dedicated to Prince Lichnowsky.*

Compared with previous works, this Sonata is remarkable as being the first example of Beethoven's use of the variation and march forms. Indeed, the work is not written in the true Sonata form, for it consists of an air with variations, a minuet, and a funeral march, concluding with a rondo. The Sonata fails in organic unity, owing to the interpolation of the funeral march, which although intrinsically a masterly work of musical art, and a worthy predecessor to the funeral march of the "Eroica" Symphony, seems as if it were "stuck into" this Sonata. It would be useless to seek for any connection between it and the other movements. What accord is there between it and the third movement which is almost volatile in character, and after the depth and grandeur of the March seems but mere confectionary? This concluding rondo—which is the weakest part of the whole work—almost jars upon us after the slow movement, the magnificent effect of which it serves to dissipate. But in proportion to the inferiority of the rondo is the superiority and beauty of the air with variations. The theme breathes an ardent longing, arising, as Marx says, out of a deep yearning, exalted feeling, "In the glorious variations," writes Marx, "this fervent feeling finds vent; it creates the variations. The first notes E, A flat inspired with this higher meaning become the motive of the first variation; the feeling intensifies and is diversified at every step, the aspiring motive is worked up higher and higher, till in the thirty-third bar from the beginning it sinks back timidly and reservedly into its native regions. Everything is resolved into motion in the second variation, in which the appearance of the theme in the tenor serves to intensify the conflict of emotions. The same impulse, though in a more fretful tone, influences the following variation, whence it naturally results that a gentle spirit of consolation, now sinking, now soaring, hovers over the next variation. The last variation gives the theme, divided alternately between the soprano and alto, in an agitated but a still more confident manner, and finishes with a sweet pleasing hushing." Beethoven treats the variation form in a totally different manner from Mozart. The latter constructs his variations merely on the formal musical foundation of the theme; with him the variation is more like an ingenious paraphrase of the form of the theme, but with Beethoven the intellectual side of the theme, and the nature of its sentiment become the ruling motive for each variation, so that a greater internal traneformation is effected. But only in the later works is this method fully developed. The scherzo of this Sonata, and the trio especially, are not devoid of considerable originality; the latter is, as Marx says, "one of those gently-breathing, self-reposeful sort of trios, such as Beethoven alone could write."

OP. 27, No. 1, E FLAT MAJOR.

Appeared about 1801. Dedicated to Princess Liechtenstein.

This Sonata is entitled "Sonata quasi una fantasia," and, both in form and matter, it is more like a fantasia than a Sonata. The strict and pure Sonata form is almost entirely laid aside, and the whole seems like a mixture of song, rondo, fantasia, and Sonata, for all these forms enter into it, and in such a manner that each has an equal and none a special prominence. Consequently, there is a want of formal organic unity, the connection between the movements appears but slight, and there is a fragmentary character about the work, as if it were an experiment in form. With this heterogeneity of expression is a want of uniformity of sentiment, and an abrupt transition from one phase of feeling to another, as in the free fantasia. There is a visible striving after a definite individual character and meaning. The first movement, andante, E flat major, $\frac{3}{4}$ time with an interlude, allegro, C major,

$\frac{6}{8}$ time, is written in the romantic style, after the manner of a song. The constant return of the theme, good as it is in itself, gives rise to a certain monotony, which requires orchestral colouring to relieve it. But what shall be said of the jovial interlude? How does it accord with the elegiac tone of the principal subject? It may be called Beethoven's humour; but to my mind it does not seem in keeping here. Whatever were Beethoven's intentions, they were not realized. And this is the case also with the incessant repetition of the chief subject which we have already noticed. One can only compare it to the second movement of Op. 90.

The second movement, allegro molto vivace, C minor, $\frac{3}{4}$ time, is not devoid of originality, with its rash, unstable, hurrying character and, in its humour it already clearly bears the stamp of the Beethoven scherzo. The third movement, adagio, A flat major, $\frac{3}{4}$ time, is cast in the true Beethoven mould and displays depth and warmth of feeling. The movement is extraordinarily short, little more than an introduction to the last, fourth movement, allegro vivace, E flat major, $\frac{2}{4}$ time—a bright, lively, agitated composition, with a dash of fantasy, almost of elfishness.

OP. 27, No. 2, C SHARP MINOR.

Composed about 1801.

Dedicated to the Countess Julie Guicciardi.

This sonata is undoubtedly one of the greatest and most important productions, not only in the circle of the Sonata, but in the whole of Beethoven's instrumental music. This work, to which the mark quasi fantasia has been attached, enjoys, in another manner, the same popularity as Op. 13. Disappointed affection was the moving cause of this composition which is dedicated "Alla Damigella Giulietta Guicciardi." "Beethoven shows," says Marx, "in his immortal C sharp minor Sonata, that love—a secret flame burning itself out in the consuming fire of insatiable desire—lived on in his true heart." Marx describes the first movement, adagio, C sharp minor $\frac{4}{4}$ time, as the song of renunciation. We hear, soft, low, plaintive tones, such as arise from the troubled and oppressed heart. The intense pain reaches a climax in the characteristic chords of the ninth in bars 16, 18, 52, 54; but closely blended with this heart-trouble is a sense of quiet submission to the inevitable, while occasionally—at the modulation into the major key—a comforting ray of light penetrates the night. With melancholy and pain the movement began, and with these it dies away. The musical colouring is bewitching, a weird, dim twilight is shed over the whole, and yet amid all the darkness and apparent confusion a definite sentiment is embodied.

An allegretto, D flat major, $\frac{3}{4}$ time, follows as the second movement. Marx says; "The song of renunciation is succeeded by the words of parting, 'Oh, think of me! I think of thee! Farewell, farewell!' uttered in fleeting, broken sobs till the last 'for ever.' Who shall pourtray the images of happy moments gone by, or the shadows of a dark future which pass before the spirit of the bereaved one in the trio?" This is an ingenious interpretation of the movement which Liszt, looking at the crashing finale that follows, calls a floweret between two abysses. But I confess, frankly, that this allegretto, with regard to the style in which it is written, the character which pervades it, and the connection in which it stands, always appears to me like an interloper. Is this really Beethoven's own style or is it that of the Haydn-Mozart Minuet? This allegretto always puts me into a mood which seems totally opposed to the sentiment which pervades the rest of the sonata. I feel a shock to my feelings in being suddenly snatched from the poetic spell of the adagio, and transported from the profoundest soul depths into a light, fleeting, easy-going sort of world. I may be mistaken so I will not seek to spoil any one else's enjoyment of this allegretto; to me, however, it is a mystery in this place, which even Marx cannot explain away.

In the last movement, presto agitato, C sharp minor, $\frac{4}{4}$ time, the spirit of the tone-poet bursts forth in gloomy passionate agitation, the pent-up wrath breaks boldly into free channels, a frightful storm begins to rage, as if some volcano were rolling out glowing lava from its thundering depths. Could this be represented more finely than in the opening motive, and in the succession of wildest harmonies and modulations which surge like tempestuous billows! The sublime spectacle of the giant's struggle with these powers of darkness is set before us, Will the struggler succumb? "No," says the second subject, that strong confident form, which appears first at bar 21, and "No" says also that flash of redeeming humour in A major, in bar 33, and afterwards in D major. Such power the demons have not gained, and there are hopeful gleams of light in the chaos. The storm may rage till the end; but it has then worn itself out, and the soul is purified, released and saved. Such is the ideal meaning of this incomparably richly coloured night piece, and we part from the work with the glad assurance that some of the truest tone-poetry has once more been vouchsafed to us.

OP. 28, D MAJOR.

Composed, 1801. *Dedicated to Joseph Edlen von Sonnenfels.*

The title "Pastorale" has been given to this Sonata. Marx expatiates on this in an ironical vein, and pointing to the Pastoral Symphony, thinks that in Beethoven's works, which bear this name aright, there is not a single repetition of a fundamental thought to be found. I do not concur in this opinion, which appears to me as true only in a certain sense, and to be taken "cum grano salis." The Sonata always awakens in my mind feelings akin to those which works like the Pastoral Symphony call forth. Is there not a gentle, fresh spring-breeze breathing through the first movement, allegro, D major, $\frac{3}{4}$ time? This is surely a sunny-bright and expressive picture of life, pleasing, richly coloured, and full of charming changes. We feel indeed that this does not exhaust the full import of the work, and that a deeper meaning lies in the whole; but the interpretation which Marx (Beethoven, vol. i. page 311, first edition) gives to the movement, and, to the whole Sonata, appears to me rather a forced one, though I agree with him, "that a hidden meaning seems to run through" the first movement. The succession of harmonies and the modulations have often a wonderful effect. Take, as one instance only, the point d'orgue on the low F sharp, in the so-called fantasia-part; "truly, thousands cannot comprehend it." This first movement is purely Beethovenish; not so those following.

The second movement, andante, D minor, $\frac{2}{4}$ time, evokes a feeling like that which comes over us when light films of cloud veil the sun, making a beautiful landscape shine in fallow light, the cloud only breaking a little now and then to admit the kindly sunbeams.

The third movement, scherzo allegro vivace, D major, $\frac{3}{4}$ time, is full of gay, teasing humour, and is characteristic through its succession of octaves, thirds, sixths, and triads; the trio again is not without originality in its obstinate repetition of a single motive. Yet the movement is only a play of sounds, and, however good as such, is not a tone-poem like the first movement.

This may be said also of the fourth movement, rondo allegro ma non troppo, D major, 6/8 time. We seem to see before us a troop of lusty sons of nature boisterously jesting and romping, seizing each other and running away, playing hide and seek, keeping as still as mice, and then bursting out and rushing on more and more joyfully and wildly. Haydn and Mozart appear very clearly—too clearly —in these last three movements, and this is one reason why there is inequality in the style of this Sonata, and the working up of the primary thought is wanting. The work always seems to me like a Janus with two faces—the one turned backwards, the other forwards.

OP. 31, No. 1, G MAJOR.
Composed about 1802.

Humour, grace, and ease are the general characteristics of the three movements of this Sonata. Marx briefly and aptly describes the first movement, allegro vivace, G major, 3/4 time, as spirited and sparkling with humour. The short chief subject has a striking effect with its incisive rhythm, and the rhythmical form implied by this motive gives to the Sonata its original character. A fine contrast is afforded by the second theme, which, full of a comfortable enjoyment, enters first in B major, and also by a third motive of a similar character, which is heard towards the end of the first part in the same key, and afterwards in G major. The whole movement is rich in surprising changes, in the bold management of the melody, harmony, and modulation, which make it extremely interesting and animated.

The second movement, adagio grazioso, C major, $\frac{9}{8}$ time, is a picture of refined, smiling gracefulness; Marx and Lenz are right in calling it idealised Italian music. In fact, Beethoven lavishly displays all sorts of sensuous charms; and yet he never loses himself in effeminacy and flabby sentimentality; never forgets that he is a German, and breathes German sincerity even into these strains. This is especially apparent in the tributary subject in A flat pp., in which the master, with a quiet, magical touch, bears us away from the laughing Hesperides, and leads us, as also in the well-devised conclusion of the movement, into real German heart-depths.

The third movement, rondo allegretto, G major, $\frac{4}{4}$ time, belongs to the prosaic type. Nothing could be more characteristic in this respect than the first subject. This theme dominates the whole of the very long movement, of which Marx says that it is possessed exclusively by a comfortable jog-trot spirit. The theme is presented with every possible variety, exhibiting inexhaustible ingenuity. But I think the master has overdone it, and has not been able to prevent a certain monotony from pervading the whole. This arises from the motive itself, which does not seem to me capable and worthy of a rich and interesting treatment. I think, too, that the composer felt this himself eventually, for, towards the end, he suddenly brings in an adagio, and then closes as suddenly with a short presto, which is in some measure a pleasant and refreshing change. Moreover, the prosaic element is, so to speak, something quite un-Beethovenish. Examined closely, the chief subject of the third movement, and several motives also of the previous movements, appear rather Mozartish in design. Altogether it conclusively appears that this Sonata, no less than its predecessor, fails in the working up of the primary thought.

OP. 31, No. 2, D MINOR.
Composed about 1802.

The first movement of this Sonata, allegro, D minor, $\frac{3}{4}$ time, is a dramatic presentation of a manly, earnest, passionate and violent conflict, accompanied by inward struggles. In the beginning of the movement, the master still betrays indecision; he pauses, reflecting whether he shall take the decisive step or not. Then, all at once, he makes up his mind and the storm bursts forth; at bar 21 the chief theme appears, as Marx says, sternly resolute and full of force, but soon joins itself to a gentler impulse of pain or of supplication; then the feeling becomes more and more restless, and the second theme has a very agitated character. Now some hard blows resound, as if the struggling spirit were bracing itself for fresh effort. Then the deep, angry, tumultuous mutterings and rollings recommence. At the beginning of the second part we hear again the largo tones; "the largo question sounds solemnly three times;" and the response is renewed, but more eager aspiration and passionate struggle. A moment's rest comes again, the largo is heard once more in a recitative full of expression, and of sorrowful submission to the inevitable. Such

I take to be the meaning of the recitative. Then the struggling and striving are renewed, till at last the storm subsides and dies away in low, gloomy mutterings.

The second movement, adagio, B flat major, $\frac{3}{4}$ time, depicts the deepest inward peace and serenest happiness. A religious feeling pervades the chief theme of this movement. But amid all this repose come occasional outbursts of passion; indescribable emotions rise and swell in the heart; an ardent yearning after higher happiness takes possession of the soul; the agitation is gently soothed, but the yearning begins again, to be, however, hushed at last. The whole is a beautiful and richly coloured piece of soul-painting.

The third movement, allegretto, D minor, $\frac{3}{8}$ time, consists properly of only two principal subjects; the first quite at the beginning of the movement of four notes only, A, F, E, D; the second of six notes at the interval of a second (F, E, F, E, F, E.) This gives a stamp of originality to the piece, especially to the second tuneless motive, and something of a bizarre tinge is imparted by the almost obstinate repetition of the theme in every key. What does this movement mean? A deep agitation runs through it; a striving after something, as there was in the first movement, but a less active striving, one might say a more resigned effort, accompanied, however, by a bitter, almost gnawing grief. Over the whole, which Marx speaks of as "perfumed with longing," there hovers a spirit of phantasy; a humorous feature runs through it, by which the former restless, and even gloomy, character of the movement is essentially modified. After careful consideration, we feel convinced that this rondo is no mere caprice, and that there is, although we may not be able to explain how, a subtle connection between it and the first movement. And the Sonata on this account gives the impression of a work uniformly carried out. It may also be noted that, according to tradition, Beethoven had a special preference for this Sonata, and frequently played it in public.

OP. 31, No. 3 E FLAT MAJOR

Composed about 1802.

The first movement, allegro, E flat major, $\frac{3}{4}$ time, begins with a short characteristic motive, such as we have already become familiar with, and which we shall find again in succeeding works. The first subject is playful and humorous, and, as it is elaborated, its facetious character predominates more and more, especially at the beginning of the second part, where, now in the treble, now in the bass, it skips about in a charming, elfish manner. The movement is formed also on a second theme which first appears in B flat major, then in E flat major. Although the first motive was very original, this has a decidedly Mozartish colouring, as its further developments show. In this movement, the independent Beethoven is clearly distinguishable from the Beethoven leaning towards Mozart.

The former meets us again in the second movement, scherzo allegro vivace, A flat major, $\frac{2}{4}$ time. This is one of the sweetest and most ætherial movements Beethoven ever wrote. One fancies one's self transported into the fantastic and humorous elfin world, into a scene in the "Midsummer Night's Dream," so magical is the spirit which pervades the composition. The charm of the colouring—the splendid and surprising effect of the alternation of forte and piano, especially the ff in F major, afterwards in D flat major—is indescribable. This movement is true fairy work.

The third movement, menuetto moderato e grazioso, E flat major, ¾ time, strongly reminds us of Mozart, so entirely is it conceived in his spirit; the trio, however, shows far more Beethovenish originality. This may be said also of the last movement, presto con fuoco, E flat major, 6/8 time, in which the climax of the humorous spirit pervading the whole Sonata is reached. This finale is formed on two short characteristic motives, one at the beginning of the movement, the other at the twelfth bar, both of which, the latter especially, are carried out in the most surprising and diversified manner. The climax is reached in the second part, where, by an enharmonic change of the G flat, F sharp major is introduced, and is further modulated into G major, the humour thus boldly and brightly expressing itself. The whole Sonata is one of the most cheerful and most free from pain which Beethoven has written; frolicksomeness and a sparkling delight in life are, to put it tersely, the characteristics of the work.

OP. 49, No. 1, G MINOR, No. 2, G MAJOR.

Composed about 1802.

There is but little to be said about these Sonatas. They are properly sonatinas, like Op. 6; though they are deeper than Op. 14. They are undoubtedly productions of Beethoven's earliest youth, and for their taking rank as Op. 49 the composer is in no way responsible. All that is worthy of notice is that the motive of the minuet in the second Sonata had already appeared in the Septett, Op. 20. This circumstance alone indicates an earlier origin for the Sonatas, for it is hardly conceivable that Beethoven should have worked out on such a small scale, a motive from one of his most important works of the first period. What connection there is resembles that between the first theme of the last movement of the "Eroica" and the pianoforte variation on it, and in another manner between the singing-theme in the Fantasia, Op. 80, and the song of joy in the Ninth Symphony; that is, a sort of preliminary study is afforded us.

OP. 53, C MAJOR.

Composed about 1803. Appeared in 1805. Dedicated to Count Waldstein.

What a giant is Beethoven in this Sonata! The first movement, allegro con brio, C major ¾ time, begins with gentle tremblings of the happiest feeling in the tone depths, embodied in a short characteristic motive. An upward impulse towards the light makes itself felt. For a moment the happy beating of the heart finds rest on a close in G. But it immediately begins again more intensely under the firm keeping of the chief motive, and passes through a short tributary movement to the second theme in the bright E major. This theme which, in contrast to the previous trembling feelings, has a firm, self-contained character, produces a delicious effect. So alluring is the spell of this motive that a host of charming forms immediately surrounds it. The tone-poet's soul is filled with the happiest, sweetest self-forgetfulness, quite given up to this beguiling fascination, absorbed as it were into this fairy world. Will it entirely lose itself? No. At the entrance of the A major, a manly self-reliant power is perceptible which, in F major, rises to a bold shout of triumph, but only to sink back again into the first delicious trembling, and then instantly to hush the most pleasing emotions till the end of the first part. With the second part that electric spark of joy in the first theme flashes forth again, and is exclusively employed in the fantasia part, till, in C major, those bright genii re-appear, exercising a yet more potent spell. They usher in the third part and the return to the first theme, with the recurrence of the same train of feelings that we had in the first part. At the entrance of the Coda, the first theme appears in the greatest intensity, the happy feeling rises to a magnificent climax, till the agitation checks itself with the chord of the dominant seventh. The bright, self-sustained form of the second theme is heard once again in the quiet depth, then another outburst of the electrical first motive, followed by rolling thunder and—all is silent. If we examine in detail the construction of this movement, we shall be astonished at the wealth of means employed, at the inexhaustible fertility of the master in ever new harmonic and rhythmical changes; in a word, at the gigantic structure which he has reared on those two motives. All possible harmonic and rhythmical means are employed—especially in the Coda—to intensify the sentiment to the utmost.

There follows, as a second movement, introduzione adagio molto, F major, $\frac{6}{8}$ time, with rondo allegretto moderato, C major, $\frac{2}{4}$ time.* The slow introduction has an aphoristic fragmentary character, and, with the exception of eight bars in the middle, which contain a deep, yearning motive, it consists, so to

---

* According to Ries, the "Andante favori pour piano," no. 35 of the works which have no opus numbers, was originally to have formed the second (middle) movement.

speak, of musical interrogations and bold, harmonious, even mystical changes, which lead to the rondo. The adagio, which Marx calls meditative, forms a striking contrast to the happy character of the preceding and following movements, and thus enhances their vivacity; so pale and wan is the colouring that it seems as if the smiling face of heaven were suddenly overcast with shadow and cloud. Then the mists suddenly disperse, and brilliant sunshine returns, when the chief theme of the rondo is heard. This motive is thoroughly imbued with the blissful spirit of the second theme in the first movement, it is at the same time very homely and simple, and even naïvely popular. The melody repeatedly returns, and so firm is its hold that it springs up ever anew, with fresh harmonic and rhythmical embellishments, always the same, yet ever in a fresh dress, it is the original theme, but adorned with delicate and exquisite figures. Suddenly from the rolling wave-like trills there arises a vigorous manly power, revealing a strong current of emotion which in A minor grows gloomy and stern. Who can tell what it is that suddenly, almost painfully, agitates the soul? Albeit, the night is but short, for the tender blissful feeling of the first theme soon comes out victoriously. Once more a violent storm arises in C minor, dark shadows close around the scene, but they also vanish. The chief theme appears again in a shortened form, but in the utmost intensity, the expression almost rising to sublimity; a moment, and the earnest feeling passes away in enchanting modulations, breathing supreme tenderness and bliss. This feeling reaches its first climax in G flat and D flat major, from which a musing train of feeling leads back to the fundamental thought. The chief theme grows more and more striking and expressive up till the arrival of the marvellous climax with the jubilant trills. This is the second climax of joyful ecstacy, the third and highest being attained in the celebrated shakes of the prestissimo which afford the clearest, most telling and most effective expression of the fundamental thought. Here is the fulfilment of what was only sought after in the C major Sonata, Op. 2, for what was only bud there is now developed into the finest blossom.

Op. 54, F MAJOR.
Composed about 1803.

This Sonata is one of Beethoven's most singular works.! Marx calls it a strange production, and apparently does not very well know what to say about it; he considers it as a mere play of sounds, not as music of the soul, much less of the mind and spirit, in which categories—(to these we shall return) —he arranges instrumental music. Lenz finds the Sonata merely bizarre, and sees in it only the weak side of the Third Period without its beauties. I must confess that the work is to me something of a riddle. I look upon it as a freak of Beethoven. The first movement, tempo di minuetto, F major, $\frac{3}{4}$ time, contains two chief themes; the first is of the quiet, cheerful, common-place type; the second, a series of octaves rushing to and fro, is rather dry and has no charm of melody. The two motives alternate and run side by side without uniting organically to form a higher whole; they seem as if they had nothing to do with each other, so entirely does each pursue its own way. If there is any leading thought, what is it? Solve the riddle who can. The movement remains an enigma to me.

The second movement, allegro, F major, $\frac{2}{4}$ time, appears to me one of the weakest which Beethoven has ever written. Can this be the Third Period? The movement consists of mere figure-work, empty and insignificant, at the most, valuable as a study.

The whole work falls coldly. The saying that "even Homer nods sometimes" would be particularly applicable, for the work shows no signs of inspiration. It must be observed, however, that, according to Schindler, this Sonata, which was printed in 1806, was written several years earlier, and before Op. 47.

OP. 57, F MINOR.

Composed, 1805. Dedicated to Count Brunswick.

The title, Appassionata, which has been given to this Sonata, is the most suitable and comprehensive which could have been chosen. In the first and third movements the work is a night piece, a picture of a violent emotional conflict, illumined, however, by bright interludes; the middle movement is an ideal flight into happier regions. The first movement, allegro assai, F minor, $\frac{12}{8}$ time, begins with one of those short characteristic themes, such as we have already frequently met with; dismal spectral shadows rise, as it were, out of the lowest depths; soft wailings issue from the heart, and fate is heard knocking at the door. Suddenly a mighty storm bursts forth, then there is a painful trembling, and in the second theme, in A flat major, there arises a wonderful sympathetic strain of happy consolation. But the storm of painful emotion begins again; there are no more interludes of light, but fits of convulsive starting; the nightly shadows assuming a firmer shape; and the agitation increasing until another climax is attained. Then there is a momentary subsidence into soft trembling tones, and that exalted spirit of strong, virile consolation gains the upper hand. But fate claims its rights, the fight must be fought out; the turmoil, therefore, is renewed. Although the voice of reconciliation is heard for the third time, the storm only rages the more vehemently; although a cheering ray of light descends from above, an almost horrible shrillness resounds from below; at the entrance of the broken chord the inward struggle rises to actual frenzy; there is a wild surging to and fro, the consoling motive even takes a gloomy character, and at last the angry thunder rolls. We have here again a thoroughly dramatic psychological picture, and the feelings that pervade it are real, heart-felt experiences.

The second movement, andante con moto, D flat major, $\frac{2}{4}$ time, forms a contrast between the beginning and concluding movements, though not in an outward, but in a deep and inward sense : it is a steadfast island between two agitated oceans. From the quiet depths there arises a holy song of blessed peace ; "a fervent supplication does this theme seem, standing firmly in the low dark depths, closely compact, full of longing, like a prayer out of the profoundest darkness." (Marx). This melody is a sunbeam full of refreshing warmth, flooding the innermost recesses of the soul, full of unending charm. How well is the soothing, woe-relieving character of the melody expressed in the modulation from the sixth to the seventh bars of the first strophe ; and then, in the second strophe, what a blissful glimpse of heaven, what quiet, happy confidence ! The variations on the theme are exquisite. They are not evolved from its formal musical structure ; but are the outcome of the ideal contents : this determines each variation. The nature of the first variation is, as Marx puts it, shy ; the theme is only repeated timidly, the melody is broken, the bass follows slowly but closely after it. In the second variation the song becomes more agitated, and is heard in a higher, brighter octave. In the third variation the expression of the theme, which is, as it were, surrounded by an accompaniment of harps, rises to pure ecstasy, the soul seems to have escaped from earth and to be bathed in the blue boundless æther. But we soon return to earth; the theme in its primal simplicity is heard again in the bass; at last it is silent, and painful strains forebode the storm of the finale. Marx describes the whole andante as a prayer full of consolation, arising out of the deepest desolation.

The third movement, allegro ma non troppo, F minor, $\frac{2}{4}$ time, begins with a succession of sixths, sounding like a wild outcry from a soul in anguish, then there is a rushing movement in the bass, like a wild mountain torrent, tearing and foaming down. The roar and ferment continue until a clear, firm form struggles out of the whirl, rushes in with wild passion, accompanied by wailing thirds ("the storm song"), the agitation ever increasing till the conclusion of the first part. The roar of the storm is renewed at the entrance of the second part, sparks of passion flash forth, and then a short tributary motive reveals poignant anguish. Now there is a distant restless surging, a mighty rolling in the depths; then the struggle becomes a little quieter, a wild whirl of octaves in C major leads to some strange convulsive startings which, at length, exhaust themselves; and in characteristic minims bring in a sudden dead silence. But only for an instant; for, at the beginning of the third part, the storm is renewed, the gloomy spectacle of the first part is repeated, and isolated flashes of light dart across the night.

At last in the Presto, the tone-poet comes forth like a warrior in armour, and with proud, virile dignity seems to say, in the full chords, "Behold! the storm has not broken the oak; it approaches again, but it will not break it now." A final storm follows, but it is powerless; the spirit has freed itself, and at last the struggle ceases in solemn minor strains. We have the assurance that the tone-poet has not succumbed to the powers of evil; he has but tried and tempered his vigorous moral strength in the conflict. A gloria song of triumph in the major key at the end would be in harmony with the motive of the whole; the conclusion must be in a strain of ardent dramatic exaltation, since the work itself is an emotional tragedy. Besides, according to Ries, this finale was conceived during a stormy night, and when Beethoven was asked by Schindler for a key to this work, and to the D minor Sonata, Op. 31, he replied: "Read Shakespeare's 'Tempest.'" We may ask, with Marx, what has that to do with it?

It is veritably a finding of the key. It is true, a Marx says, that much of what is called fantasy is to be found in this work, especially in the first movement; but we must add that it is a fantasy bounded and governed by reason and force of will, a fantasy in which are represented the unfathomable depths of the human heart.

OP. 78, F SHARP MAJOR.
Composed 1809. Dedicated to the Countess Brunswick.

The first movement, adagio cantabile, and allegro ma non troppo, F sharp major, $\frac{2}{4}$ time and $\frac{4}{4}$ time, begins with a motive full of deep yearning, is truly Beethovenish, as is the chief theme of the allegro which follows it. But the continuation does not fulfil the expectations that we have raised, for the movement loses in substance, and fritters itself away in a play of sounds devoid of any deeper meaning. Still more decidedly is this the case with the second movement, allegro vivace, F sharp major, $\frac{2}{4}$ time. It is needless to waste many words over this when we are still under the influence of the impression left by the F minor Sonata. Marx even passes over this Sonata in silence, and Lenz says, simply and pertinently, "Beethoven's hand has worked at it, but not his genius."

OP. 79, G MAJOR.

Appeared 1810. *Date of composition uncertain.*

The last remark is still more emphatically applicable to this Sonatina, as the work is called. It is without doubt a youthful production like the Sonatas, Op. 49. The opus number 79 has neither rhyme nor reason. One would rather have supposed Haydn to be the composer, had not Beethoven been named as such. The work must surely have been published afterwards as a stop-gap. For the use and edification of those who are interested even in this trifle of the great Beethoven, we will again quote Marx, who says the Sonatina presents a "presto alla tedesca," superficial but lively (if only the second part of the cuckoo-like concluding movement were not so very tame), a short and essentially small andante, G minor, and a joyful Viennese-like finale.

OP. 81, E FLAT MAJOR.

Composed 1809. *Dedicated to the Archduke Rudolph.*

This is the first and only Sonata by Beethoven which has a definite programme to indicate its contents. This consists of three words : "Les adieux, l'absence, et le retour"—farewell, absence, and return. Thus the Sonata has become one of the most understandable among the later works of the master. The first movement, adagio, ¾ time, then allegro, ¼ time, E flat major, begins with the word of parting, "lebewohl," (farewell) enunciated by the first three crotchets, and painful feelings pass through the loving heart; at first it is an anxious presentiment of parting (Marx), but with the entrance of the allegro comes the anguish of the actual separation, though it is not a hopeless grief nor a trouble unaccompanied by a certain happy sense of exaltation. It seems to me that in this allegro here are, so to speak, three moods and three phases of feeling which, in consequence of the approaching separation from a beloved object, spontaneously appear in wonderful unison; the painful sense that after all there must be a parting; the excited ardent feeling of parting from an object worthy of such sorrow; and the consolatory assurance that the separation is not final. The motive at the beginning of the movement seems to me to correspond to the first, the octave motive which soon follows to the second, and the later motive, marked expressivo, to the third phase of feeling, while again the descending motive, at the conclusion of the first part, strikingly expresses quiet submission to the inevitableness of the parting.

At the beginning of the second part the first state of feeling has the upper hand for some time in a varied and characteristic form; then the other two re-appear; at last however, everything is concentrated in the most impressive manner into the simple earnest expression of farewell; and there follows, towards the end of the movement, the ardent and bitter-sweet embrace of the beloved object—and the parting moment arrives. Extreme upholders of the abstract laws of harmony and of the requirements for tuneful effect, such as Fétis and Oulibicheff, are, of course, shocked that Beethoven should have suffered the chords, E flat and G, B flat and F, to be heard in succession; but in this case the higher law of ideality prevails. "Beethoven," says Marx, tersely and pertinently, "was not dealing with chords, but depicting a fond farewell, and as was ever the case with him the ideal over-ruled the material." Beethoven and the mere musician do not always go the same way. "Notes or chords are as little the essence of music as words are of poetry; the genius of the poet forms and fashions both to his own ends." (Marx). In a word, sound and harmony are here made subservient to ideal representation.

The second movement, andante expressivo, C minor, 2/4 time, pictures the feelings of the friend who is left in loneliness. Marx says, very justly, that the whole character of the movement shows itself in the first few bars, in the dragging march of the bass, and in the alternate impulses of attraction and repulsion which characterise the treble. But this feeling of desolation is accompanied by an ardent longing for the return of the absent one; what else does that expressive melody say to us, which appears first in D major, then in C major?

And now the return—the meeting—these are pourtrayed in the third movement, vivacissime, E flat major, 6/8 time. The friend is coming—go to meet him—so say the first notes, and so says the stormy rush of the semi-quavers. At the entrance of the chief motive all the pulses of life beat more quickly, and the meeting is celebrated right jubilantly. The overflowing delight now yields to a quiet contained ecstacy (the motive in crotchets) which, however, at the entrance of the G flat major, immediately changes into sweet smiles of exquisite delight, into caressing kisses of supremest joy. All these varying expressions of rapture recur, but in every fresh musical dress there is an incessant repetition of the jubilant song of meeting. Then when these feelings have had full and free vent, the sentiment suddenly becomes more collected, (poco andante) devout, and touchingly expressive; for, as Marx well says, it would be impossible that emotion should not mingle with the joy of the happy ones. They embrace once more, but with what different feelings than when they parted, for now both feel secure in the assurance of everlasting union. In this harmonious spirit the work closes, and this impression rests with the hearer afterwards. The theory of the "two principles" mentioned in reference to op. 14 is applicable in a very different and much greater degree to this Sonata. In the first and third movements there are really two distinct intellectual personalities, there is an actual dialogue. To find out who it is intended to represent is quite superfluous, and would not enhance the ideal meaning of the work. Enough, if we know—as goes, without saying—that Beethoven is one person; whether the other form be that of friend or lady-love is immaterial. Especially to be noted, is the masterly power with which the different feelings in this Sonata are welded together into a close ideal unity, so that as by a psychological necessity they develop one out of another.

OP. 90, E MINOR.

Composed 1814   Dedicated to Count Maurice Lichnowsky.

Just as clearly and definitely as the idea of the work appeared in the last-named Sonata, equally difficult is it to indicate it even with the least approach to certainty in the E minor Sonata. Marx felt this when he said that it was one of those pictures which seem to look at us with inquiring questioning glances; they are going to speak out quite clearly and—words fail them ; as if our art had periods, when it is, as it were, suspended between mere sound and definite expression, when one expects every moment to hear the solving word, but it is always withheld. The Sonata is dedicated to Count Lichnowsky. The latter is said to have asked Beethoven what the idea of the work was, and that he replied, amid roars of laughter, that he had intended to set to music the love story between the Count and his wife—a public dancer—and that he should write over the first movement, "struggle between head and heart"; and over the second, "conversation with the beloved one." Marx was certainly right in regarding this answer of Beethoven's as a joke, for it gives no clue to the meaning of the composition. Though the intention of this

Sonata cannot be so clearly expressed in words as it can in other works, yet the tone-language is not wanting in individuality and character. We subscribe entirely to what Marx says of the first movement, E minor, 3/4 time—Beethoven has written over it "with life, and with feeling and expression throughout," instead of putting any fixed tempo mark)—that it reveals a noble mind and energetic character, and shows what the force of eloquence can do in combating distressing doubts and fears. "A restless aspiration—that is always encountering obstacles, but never quite exhausted, though it often timidly retreats in despair—an alternation of resolution and yielding, of pressing forward and drawing back—such is the character of the whole movement." (Marx). The aim is not attained, and the soul has a foreboding of this while it struggles; the tone, therefore, often rises to poignancy and painful bitterness, but at the end the trouble seems to disappear in quiet submission to the inevitable. The formal musical construction of the movement is masterly, a production of the utmost artistic ripeness, exquisitely finished even to the smallest details.

The second movement, E major, 2/4 time, with the

direction "to be played very singingly and not too fast," now flows on quietly and restfully in its rondo-song-like-form. It opens with a rich, melodious theme, full of earnestness, which, after the fashion of the rondo, constantly returns after short interruptions, during which the most varied and joyful images hover, as it were, around the chief figure till at last the whole softly and tenderly dies away. The movement gives the impression of a heart-idyll. As Marx says, it certainly has no fresh ideas or aspects. But in the limited sphere which in comparison to the first this movement affords, the mind feels a sense of happiness and of contentment which restores its peace. Such seems to me the meaning of this movement, with which the Sonata closes; though the feelings which it pourtrays do not convey that sense of satisfaction which we previously felt. Yet who would question their justifiableness? Do they not follow as a sort of psychological necessity from the character of the first movement? The law of raising the sentiment to a climax, in the sense in which we usually take it, is not indeed carried out in this sonata; but this is not an absolute authoritative law for all occasions; it has, like every other law, exceptions founded on the character of the particular work, and the Sonata before us is surely such an exception.

OP. 101, A MAJOR.

Composed, 1813. *Dedicated to the Baroness Erdmann.*

This Sonata, also, belongs to those works whose meaning is more or less lost in words, and can only be suggested. Marx says, "The innermost and most secret stirrings of a tender soul, to whom the desire alone is granted, not its realisation, only the flights of fancy, not tangible aims or pithy deeds—how difficult is it to catch what it says, and to bring it to a light that shall not offend it." The first movement, allegretto ma non troppo, ("rather lively and with the warmest feeling," as Beethoven has marked it) A major, $\frac{6}{8}$ time, bears the character of fervent yearning, now timid and now bold. Towards what is the desire directed? Who can explain it? A feeling of mystery runs through these strains, and they are, at least, the product of an intense individualism. Marx finds in them nervous agitation, and even breathlessness. I do not agree with him, for, to my mind, the Sonata is too ideally, and imaginatively conceived, for such to be the case; nor is it in accordance with this, when Marx immediately afterwards finds in the movement "the reserve and speechlessness of Ottilie, without the storms through which this most pleasing of Goethe's creations passes." The fantasia style, though of course not in the confused sickly manner of later composers, predominates decidedly in the second movement, vivace alla marcia, F minor, $\frac{4}{4}$ time. Marx remarks very pertinently of this movement in the march form: "Actual deeds are not represented here, but the imagination of deeds which may happen, dreamed-of strokes of bold and lofty heroism." The effect is almost ætherial, so light, undulating and bright, though not without a certain grandeur; we do not so to speak meet with the tangible, material side of the march measure, which is made subservient to the ideal expression. The rhythmical and tonal effects are of the most original kind. As instances of the former, Marx brings forward the jerky character of the chords, with their wide skips and abrupt intervals; regarding the latter, we need but refer to the frequent simultaneous sounding of the highest and lowest register without the interposition of the middle one. The tributary movement, in B flat, after the manner of a trio, with its smooth wave-like effects forms a beautiful rhythmical contrast to the march.

Following as a third movement, is a short adagio ma non troppo ("slowly and yearningly,"), A minor, $\frac{3}{4}$ time. A dull sorrow, a gentle complaining, and then again a painful yearning, breathe through these strains. Who satisfies this longing? And how can it be satisfied? The feelings which we experienced in the first movement take possession of the soul again. And now behold a new quick spirit springs up as it were by magic. Its meaning is confident self-reliance, and buoyant resolution.

In this spirit the fourth movement begins, allegro, (" quickly, but not too fast, and with decision," says the master), A major, $\frac{3}{4}$ time. The character of buoyant resolution could not be more strikingly represented than by the first subject with its distinctive rhythm. The theme enters in harmony, indeed in double counterpoint, and is very brisk and animated. After an earnest, expressive motive (dolce) the second subject is heard, which strikes a child-like, cheerful chord of nature. And when the fugue in A minor begins, a humorous feeling makes itself felt. As regards its formal musical construction we find with an exact imitation of the melody, every possible inversion, and the most surprising combinations. At length on the point d'orgue, in the dominant E, there is a return to the first subject, and the same succession of gladdest resolution, child-like, naive joy, and humour is heard again. The latter struggles out alone at last and asserts itself triumphantly. Marx says of the whole movement : a rich, refreshing stream of life over which brilliant gleams occasionally flash gaily, courageously and impetuously gushes forth." This sonata is, as we soon discover, a very uniformly sustained work. As regards the formal construction, it is, as was pointed out in the second movement, and is true more or less of the whole work—the peculiar cast of the rhythm which rivets attention.

OP. 106, B FLAT MAJOR.

Composed 1818.   Dedicated to the Arch-Duke Rudolph.

The grandest Sonata ever composed, of colossal dimensions, a real giant, symphonically conceived and framed throughout. The first movement, allegro, B flat major, $\frac{3}{4}$ time, is constructed on two themes ; the first displaying manly boldness, power, pride, decision, and magnanimity : the second, womanly gentleness, grace, tenderness, softness and devotion. The first subject opens the movement with a full chord in marked rhythm, its instant repetition a third higher, showing the ruling character only the more forcibly. A tributary subject—the very embodiment of gentleness—then appears; it is repeated an octave higher and thus becomes the more effective. A noble, manly power then bursts forth in full chords, the progress of the movement is carried on with true grandeur, a majestic descent of octaves from the high C follows, and a corruscation of brilliancy flashes from the broken notes of the F major chord, on which the figure of the first theme again finds a firm footing. The striking modulation into D brings about the transition to the second subject in G major, which now displays itself in the most charming changes, and assumes the most winning forms. But see, it yields at last to an aspiring tone figure (entrance of the C major), from which again there arises an earnest yearning song (the motive, cantabile dolce ed expressivo), but only to yield immediately to the powerful impetuous spirit of the first theme. Thus the first part concludes. With the second part, a new scene of a very tensive character presents itself, rhapsodical figures produce a highly expectant feeling, the key changes to E flat major, the trumpet-call sounds once and again. What does it herald? The first theme, which appears in the quiet depth, and gradually rises higher and higher to a wonderful climax, which is at last reached in the bright D major; then those strains of deep, mournful yearning are heard again, but the first theme returns, and at the beginning of the third part, marches boldly forth once more, fully equipped, but accompanied with still richer ornament. The configuration and sentiment of the first part re-appear, but in a new, original and loftier style. Bold beyond measure is the modulation into C flat after the violent surging to and fro in broken octaves, and, after the last out-breathings of that spirit of yearning, the sentiment gathers itself, as it were, into a focus with the return of the first subject, which, in a shortened form, gradually dies away; its expression is essentially modified, so that it seems as if vigour and gentleness, power and tenderness, after separately developing themselves in a dramatic struggle, were at the end reconciled and closely united. We might say, with the poet; "Wo Starkes sich mit Mildem paaret, da giebt es einen guten Klang." What other first movement of a Sonata can show such wonderful proportions?

The second movement, scherzo, B flat major, $\frac{3}{4}$

time, displays a restless, unstable character, a strange hurrying, a peculiar hunting, fleeing, and crowding; in the chief movement, especially, an unsatisfied longing, but in the so-called trio, B minor, in the following presto, and at the conclusion, a picture of bold, fantastic bizarre humour is depicted, reminding us of the wonderful, strange colouring in the B flat minor movement. Lenz's remark, that this movement recalls Goethe's words in "Faust:"

> "Was weben die dort um den Rabenstein?
> Schweben auf, schweben ab, neigen sich, beugen sich.
> Vorbei! Vorbei!"

seems to me very pertinent. The formal construction is particularly interesting, inasmuch as in the principal movement, we meet, with a rhythm of seven bars twice over, then four bars twice, and so seven and eight alternately. This serves but to heighten the originality.

The third movement, adagio sostenuto, (appassionato e con molto sentimento), F sharp minor, $\frac{6}{8}$ time, is a painful, ardent, yearning prayer for light and joy, out of profound sorrow and darkness; a tone-poem pervaded by real religious inspiration and devotion. What could be more expressive than the upward impulse in the first subject, issuing from the innermost heart! At the entrance of the G major, the first joyful beam of heavenly light penetrates the night, but all is immediately dark again. Gleams of joy break through in F sharp major, and now, when the low D is heard, then the low F sharp, and when this progression is repeated in the treble, what comforting, hopeful restfulness breathes in these sounds! We might here again say with the poet, "was des Mannes Brust ernst und tief beweget"; it is that which is expressed. Darkness, which the exalted forms of light vainly endeavour to pierce, again covers all; for a long time despair and gloom hold fatal sway. But those deep unfathomable strains in F sharp major are heard again, and produce a sense of bliss, which is heightened by a magical modulation from E flat to F sharp. With the change into G major, that well of comfort is drawn from for the last time, the primary feeling then returns. The grief gradually subsides, but the darkness and horror of the night are not to be banished by the penetrating beams of the morning sun; it is only the glimmer of the stars which falls from heaven, yet it pours a wonderful tranquility into the soul. Simple and intelligible, with all their grandeur, as are the lofty ideal contents of this the most gigantic adagio of pianoforte music, equally clear and simple is its formal construction. At the first glance this might appear otherwise; but closer consideration makes visible the lightest architectural grouping. Certainly everything is broadly and massively planned, like the first movement, for the giant's limbs have other proportions than those of ordinary men; but although huge they are shapely, and possess real beauty, symmetry and harmony. So it is with this movement, the simple form of which is: A, chief subject, F sharp minor—Trio, D major—Fantasia; B, chief subject with variations, F sharp minor, D major—Trio F sharp minor—Coda F sharp minor. We have here a peculiar union of the Sonata and Rondo form. Before we leave the movement it may be mentioned, as worthy of note, that, according to Ries, the two notes of the first bar were written by Beethoven afterwards. The two low bass notes came in apparently in the course of the movement, with the closer management of the chief theme, which begins strictly in the second bar; their great importance became evident to the master, and he thus recognised and supplied the want at the beginning of the movement. Lenz says, they seem like two steps towards the grave's gate, and describes the movement as an unmeasured wail over the ruin of all happiness.

The fourth movement is opened by an introduction, largo, B flat major, $\frac{4}{4}$ time, in a free, rhythmical, harmonious form. As a recitative full of meaning, this highly poetic, almost dramatic, prelude, is powerfully effective, stirring, as Marx says, all the regions of the tone world. But who can explain this tone-mystery any further? Enough if we feel the grandeur of the master's imagination, if we recognise that we have not before us a mere conglomeration of notes and play of sounds, but that a deeper meaning runs through all. These words apply also to that which follows the largo, the great three-part fugue, allegro resoluto, B flat major, $\frac{3}{4}$ time, in which Marx perceives the expression of a most deeply agitated spirit, restlessly swaying to and fro, coloured, softened, and restrained by certain elegiac tones. A representation of supreme unrest is set before us, so gloomy often that one fancies it is a storm with fiery lightnings and rolling thunder, conjured up by unknown forces, an unchaining of the dark powers. Isolated gleams of light shine through, now and then, and a humorous impulse is often distinctly heard. Certain it is that highly individualised feelings rest in the back-ground, and are very hard to explain; as, indeed, in respect to form, this fugue is one of the most difficult exercises of musical art, for the form, modulation, and working out of the themes are so peculiar that the whole is by no means easy to follow; properly speaking, it is rather a strange union of the fugue and rondo forms than a pure strict fugue; but the movement does not, on this account, stand any-the-less on an equality with Bach's creations, for contrapuntal art and freedom; only with this difference, that the spirit of the nineteenth century here pervades the form.*

In conclusion, a word from Marx on the whole work: "Both in external proportions and in depth of meaning, the tone-poem far over-passes the boundaries which even Beethoven himself had hitherto reached in pianoforte music." The uniform bond which unites the four movements of the Sonata is, in my opinion, the ideal grandeur of the conception and execution; the work bears throughout the stamp of originality and boldness. It might be difficult to prove that the different movements follow each other as a psychological necessity.

---

* Lenz calls the Fugue: "cauchemar" and "rudis indigestaque moles!"

OP. 109, E MAJOR.
Composed about 1814. Dedicated to Miss Brentano.

The first movement of this Sonata, in which a vivace ma non troppo, E major, $\frac{3}{4}$ time, alternates with an adagio expressivo, $\frac{2}{4}$ time, begins very simply but very significantly. The freest and most natural harmony plays around these fleeting, hovering strains, and the soul appears to lose itself in a fairy dream-world. Sometimes the waves seem to rise higher, but they subside again, and the stream of sounds glides on gently and tranquilly. Grave tones are heard in the adagio; "a sharp pain," says Marx, "like a stab at the heart," transfixes the gentle being, and is followed by a strong ebullition of feeling; this figure of gloom appears twice, but the lovely images of the dream always regain the mastery, and only hover around the soul the more deliciously. Who can say of what peculiar state of feeling this is the outcome? There is something fanciful about the whole plan and construction of the movement; despite its depth of feeling it gives the impression of a free fantasia rather than of a movement in the strict Sonata-form. Marx points out, as specially significant, the chorale-like succession of chords towards the end. Even Lenz cannot understand this movement; he calls it inconceivably weak and attenuated.

The second movement, prestissimo, E minor, $\frac{6}{8}$ time, bears the character of intense dissatisfaction, of miserable, restless pressing, of a dark pursuing, involuntarily reminding us of the furies chasing Orestes; indeed, now and then we think of Faust's words as he becomes blind: "Was schwebet schattenhaft heran?" This latter allusion applies only to the motive in octaves, which is heard at bar 25, and to the gleams of light, which first appear at 51 and following bars, and then flit here and there like an ignis fatuus. Marx finds in the movement the foreboding and the agony of death. The sentiment depicted is an almost nervous one, highly agitated, and intensely sensitive, yet not morbid. As regards the formal construction, many will be reminded of the later Mendelssohnian manner; just as the March in the A major Sonata, Op. 101, recalls, in some portions of the second part, Berlioz and Wagner. The construction as well as the character of the movement is fantasia-like throughout.

The third movement, andante molto cantabile ed expressivo, E major, $\frac{3}{4}$, $\frac{9}{8}$, and $\frac{4}{4}$ time, is a theme with variations. The air comes in quietly, but firmly, decidedly, and at the same time very simply; it is a song of deep feeling, an emanation of sincere, true restfulness of soul, a happy submission to destiny; such is the feeling it evokes. Marx calls the theme "one of those melodies full of holy devotion, in which the soul, in deep abstraction, reflects on the past; does not think, but with the images of the past reflected as in a crystal-clear stream, falls into a reverie with many an afterthought, and many a sigh, and," continues Marx, "thus far Beethoven, the poet; Beethoven, the musician, has written the variations; they are very pretty." On a close and thorough examination of these variations, and a comparison of them with others, for example with Op. 57, I agree with Lenz that the ideal contents of the theme certainly do not appear as the sole spring and centre of the variations; its character seems more or less effaced; this work is, accordingly, to be judged from the point of view of formal musical construction. The variations, however, are of themselves among the most charming which Beethoven has written; in the last variations, especially, enchanting strains are heard, sparks of humour flash forth. The theme in its original form beautifully concludes the whole.

OP. 110, A FLAT MAJOR.
Composed, 1821.

The opening of the first movement moderato cantabile molto expressivo, A flat major, ¾ time, is only to be described as "freundlich-hold" (amiably lovely); it has a distant assonance with the motive of the canon in the second finale of Mozart's "Cosi fan tutti." After a close, a song of deep even ardent yearning commences; then suddenly, harp-like strains are heard, and the most laughing images flit around the soul. Happy forms arise in gay multiplicity, that song of yearning and the first motive which in the so-called fantasia part is so conspicuous re-appear. The picture is richly coloured and the sense of cessation is very finely depicted in bars 6 and 13 before the end to which the immediately preceeding and subjoined harp lispings afford an effective contrast. Marx finds in the movement the parting from a beloved instrument in an Ossian-like sense. Who would dispute that a touch of deep sadness prevails throughout?

There follows as a second movement, allegro molto, F minor, ¾ time, which is a scherzo both in form and character. We meet again, although in another form, the same wild hurrying, and anxious hunting and crowding as in the scherzi of some of the last named Sonatas. Marx points out as significant the resemblance in bar 8 of the second clause to a wild popular song, "Ich bin lüderlich, du bist lüderlich," and asks, "Did there then ever come over the pure singer a dissatisfaction with the life that he was leading, a scorn of the foolish play which they call life?" How fine, in contrast to the wild almost frenzied character of this movement, is the middle movement in D flat major, the so-called trio! How fantastic and aerial, how interwoven with bright streaks of light! And how expressive is the Coda with those full powerful chords, separated by pauses which only make them the more impressive, and the final gentle dying away in the major!

The third movement is introduced by an adagio ma non troppo, B flat minor, $\frac{4}{4}$ time, very solemn and grave, interwoven with a recitative full of unspeakable secret woe, which at last finds vent in a tender arioso, E flat minor, $\frac{12}{16}$ time. In this plaintive song, the soul fully but quietly pours out all its sorrow.

But this repose is abandoned for life and activity in the fourth movement, fuga, allegro ma non troppo, A flat major, 6/8 time. The agitation subsides at the re-entrance of the arioso, which at first expresses a yet deeper mourning and breathes more profound sighs; but, after a masterly transition, the stirring figures of the fugue again "weben hin, weben her, fluthen hin, fluthen her," with ever-increasing energy to the end, where the sweeping harp-like strains are again heard—a clever imitation, an expressive souvenir of the spirit of the first movement, but, at the same time, an artistic conclusion of the whole. Strongly individual states of feeling must have inspired this Sonata. In it Beethoven's tone-language becomes more and more subjective, if not obscure, and sometimes mysterious; any explanation in words can give but a suggestion as to the meaning which grows increasingly difficult. A certain reserve is advisable if we would not lose ourselves in capricious phantasmagoria. Instrumental music often offers riddles, which perhaps will never be fully solved, as the next and last of Beethoven's Sonatas gives reason to observe.

OP. 111, C MINOR.

Composed 1822.   Dedicated to the Archduke Rudolph.

The first movement commences with a maestoso in C minor, ¾ time. What Titanic power! What a volcanic outburst! Powerful, solemn, majestic, impressive, how much more full of meaning is this Introduction than that to the "Sonata Pathétique!" The skips of a seventh in the first bars show, in a masterly manner, the deep laceration of the heart; the modulations beginning in the sixth bar have a wonderfully relieving, soothing effect; marvellously original and drastic is the change to the allegro con brio ed appassionato, C minor, ¾ time, which is like the distant roll of the thunder coming nearer and nearer, or the howling of the wind. The chief theme then bursts forth, a sombre image of passionate agitation and bold defiance. With wild impetuosity the storm pursues its resistless course, the momentary abatement in the passages marked poco ritenuto only producing a yet more violent outburst. With the appearance of the A flat major wild sparks of humour flash forth, and then the spirit suddenly soars into a freer, lighter sphere, but only for an instant to brace itself anew for a sterner struggle. Terrible is the fury of the storm in the second part, yet out of the night the soul again struggles forth and once more soars happily heavenwards, in the clear C major. A last foaming of the dark billows, then a gradual subsidence of the dashing waves, and "tiefe Stille herrscht im Wasser, ohne Regung ruht das Meer." Just as the matter of this movement is superbly grand, so is its formal construction simplicity itself, being nothing but the two-part Sonata-form. It affords a striking illustration of how the greatest ends are attainable with the smallest means.

The second and last movement opens with an arietta adagio molto semplice cantabile, C major, $\frac{9}{16}$ time, a song-like theme (Marx says, popular song) followed by four variations which resolve themselves into a sort of fantasia, to which is coupled a new variation of the air, connected with which is a tributary movement, which, uniting shakes and bass figures to the first eight bars of the theme, brings in a coda and conclusion. Such, in bare words, is the simple formal process, the skeleton, so to speak, of the movement, but what about the contents? Kullak says that the Sonata sinks into insipidity in the variations. Lenz thinks that strange and marvellous ideas had been projected, but that the arietta, that divine exhalation, lamentably loses itself in running figure work; finally, Marx says, the arietta with the strangely dissevered melodies, with the deep descending bass, with the change into A minor, with the repetition of the emphasized notes E... E... recalls those elegiac melodies, the funeral songs. Marx then continues: "Variations carry out the suggestions of the arietta; who can say all, and who can explain all?" "I have hidden much therein," Goethe once said, in a similar case. Elsewhere Marx speaks of the composition as a theme of deep feeling, overflowing with tender, profound melancholy, developed with the utmost regularity but with ever increasing richness, now subdued, now pleasantly stirred, but returning to the elegiac primary tone of feeling, then rousing up with new courage, and afterwards sinking into the deepest despondency. It is quite inconceivable to me how Kullak can feel any insipidity in these strains, and for the same reason also I can but pity Lenz's regret, for both seem to me only to have grasped the shell, without penetrating to the kernel. On the other hand, one can agree with Marx that Beethoven has "hidden much" in this movement. I cannot describe the impression which it always makes upon me. It seems as if we had an echo from the loftiest ideal and spiritual regions, the language, which is simply untranslatable into words, of the soul soaring to the heavenly regions with fervent and holy rapture. When I thus completely lose myself in this tone-world, the last scene of the second part of Goethe's "Faust"—Faust's transfiguration—always occurs to me. We may find in the second strophe of the arietta, "Zeugen menschlicher Bedürftigkeit," "Spuren von schroffen Erdenwegen," but only "dass ja das Nichtige Alles verflüchtige"; such is the tendency of this tone-creation. How wonderfully does the deep, fervent song of the arietta ever aspire towards the heavenly spheres, just as Faust was ever lifted higher—"steigt hinan zu höherem Kreise." In fancy one sees the hovering forms of the pater profundus, pater seraphicus, and pater ecstaticus, when, full of the fantasy of the tone-poem, we follow it, now into the lowest, then into the highest tone-regions. Towards the end does not a feeling take possession of us akin to that of the angel's song in the lines:

> "Nebelnd um Felsenhöh—spür ich so eben
> Regend sich in der Näh—ein Geisterleben.
> Die Wölkchen werden klar: ich seh' bewegter Schaar,
> Seliger Knaben,—los von der Erde Druck,
> Im Kreis geselt— die sich erlaben
> An neuem Lenz und Schmack—der obern Welt.

If it be said to me, "You are writing mere idle fancies," I certainly cannot produce proof to the contrary, but it will at least be granted that I only write what I truly feel. And is it, then, so incredible that there should be a point of contact betwen the greatest of German word-poets, and the greatest of German tone-poets? Enough if it be but admitted that here, as in all deep instrumental music, there lies a mystery, a mystery which always reveals itself more or less according to the nature of the imagination that contemplates it. Without imagination no musical work can be understood, least of all a creation of Beethoven's; mere musical knowledge, mere acquaintance with the laws of composition do not suffice.* To return once more and finally to the second movement of the Sonata; these are no ordinary variations. They were not written by Beethoven the musician, but by Beethoven the tonepoet; they are creations such as he alone could produce, such, for example, as he has given us in the Sonata, Op. 57. Kullak says in the work from which we have already quoted that "the variations fail in that lofty intellectual development which

---

* We might say as Beethoven himself did about his music: "thousands do not understand it.'

cannot endure the monotony of repetition except as a brief relaxation from a lyrical strain; the variations have no leading thought and no vital energy, for which reason they should have been placed in the middle, not at the end of a great work." Whatever else of truth these words may contain, they do not apply to the variations in question. Variations such as Op. 111 are like an ideal emanation of the theme, or, to use a simile, are the pure rays radiating from the theme, enthroned like a sun in a firmament of supernal peace. These variations are but a deeper and more spiritual expression of the theme. The formal aspect of the variation retreats, and the free, spontaneous play of imagination creates an ideal dénouement. Do not these so-called variations form a satisfactory conclusion? Is a concluding movement still wanting? Schindler says, yes; that he asked the master why he did not write a third movement, corresponding to the first two, and Beethoven replied that time failed him for a third movement; he was therefore obliged to expand the second. Believe this who will. Could Beethoven have found time to give this extension to the second movement if it had failed him for a third? A pretty contradiction. And even if Beethoven did give utterance to this speech, it is well-known how laconic his answers often were, and how promptly he cut short inquisitive, intrusive questioners. Perhaps he thought, too, with Mephistopheles, "Das Beste was du weisst, darfst du den Buben doch nicht sagen." I consider that a third movement was psychologically as impossible as a tenth symphony.

As Gervinus says, after a discussion of Shakespeare's latest work, so we say, with the C minor Sonata Beethoven finished his course as a Sonata-maker, and, like Prospero, broke and buried fathoms deep the magic wand of his tone-poetry. Happy the disciple who recovers this treasure.

No one has yet found it, notwithstanding the great achievements of Franz Schubert and others, and the Beethoven Sonata stands, unrivalled in original beauty, an inexhaustible well of the purest wonderment, a glittering crown of stars to all who seek after pure musical forms.

FIFTH PART.

Retrospective.—Concluding Remarks.

IF we now glance over the rich world which the Beethoven Sonatas reveal to us, we shall see that these fall naturally into several groups. We meet with works which evidently belong to Beethoven's early youth; with works in which, although riper, the influence of Beethoven's predecessors, Haydn and Mozart, is still dominant; with works in which Beethoven's independence becomes paramount, and the Haydn-Mozart influence vanishes; and finally with works in which Beethoven appears in his complete individuality, the former foundations having entirely disappeared. The groups will then be as follows:

GROUP I.—Op. 6, 49, 79.
GROUP II.—Op. 2, 7, 10, 13, 14, 22.
GROUP III.—Op. 26, 27, 28, 31.

GROUP IV.—Op. 53, 54, 57, 78, 81, 90, 101, 106, 109, 110, 111.

But the last five works of group IV., belonging to Beethoven's so-called Third Period, are so essentially different from the others, that they might lay claim to an independent subdivision and group. There would thus be comprised in

GROUP V.—Op. 101, 106, 109, 110, 111.

Before characterising and analysing these groups, we would state emphatically that it is not our intention to set up lifeless limitations, but to seek some landmarks in this rich and vast musical domain. If we keep in mind that it is not necessary to force any work into a barren category, if we recognise that the groups are themselves united together by delicate threads—for the succeeding always rests its basis on the preceding one—a certain systematic arrangement will serve to distinguish a particular work, and set it in a more characteristic light.

With respect to the different groups, group 1 certainly needs no further consideration. As general characteristics of the works of the second group, besides the basis of the Haydn-Mozart style of writing, the following may be mentioned; concerning the substance, a leading, poetical, fundamental idea is still more or less wanting, and this deficiency pervades the character of the works which have least meaning and purpose; concerning the form, it has been prevailingly prompted by mere custom; the relation of the keys is often the only bond between the movements and the only means by which a similar and uniform character is imparted to the whole. The so-called second subject still occupies, as with Mozart, a great deal of space, makes its independance felt, while in the more perfect later works the first subject is the decisive part of the movement, the second theme yielding to it in importance, by which means a much closer unity is attained.

The most important work of this group, in many ways stretching far beyond it, and in parts even surpassing works of the third group, is undoubtedly the D major Sonata, Op. 10. In group III. there appear so many waverings and leanings towards Haydn and Mozart (for example, Op. 26, 28, 31^1, 31^3), that single movements might still be ranked in the second group; but the intellectual basis of the works generally is a higher one, a definite poetical meaning comes out more clearly, the short characteristic chief motive of the works of the following group appears. The most prominent work of the third group is indisputaably, the C sharp minor Sonata, which, with the exception of the second movement, might certainly be placed in the next group. The following characteristic signs appear in the works of the fourth group: The uniform, definite purport of the Sonata; the short, characteristic chief subject; the exclusive employment of the latter in the so-called fantasia part; the working-up of the chief theme in the Coda, which obtains thereby a certain independence and exclusiveness; the limitation of the second thought to its place in the first, and repetition in the so-called third part; the general abandonment of the four and even three-movement form, with the predominance of the two-movement form; and the more symphonic character of the Sonata, that is as regards the form and working out of the idea, not with respect to its conception and to the polyphonic character of the symphony, for the Sonatas are of purely homophonic form.

The most valuable work of this group is the Sonata, Op. 57, while the Sonatas, Op. 54, and Op. 78, properly belong to it only on account of their formal construction; in matter they are far surpassed by works of earlier groups.

Finally, concerning group V., the peculiarities of

the works belonging to it are: the appearance of the polyphonic, contrapuntal element; the return to the three and four-movement form; the disappearance of the two-movement form (except in Op. 111); the resumption of the small sonatina and march form; and the highly individual subjective contents.

The fugue form is more freely and fancifully treated than with Bach; it may be called a blending of the fugue and rondo forms, in which charming tributary movements ever and anew animate the cold fugue form, although we must also admit that a certain amount of harshness is perceptible. The abandonment of the two-movement form in the first four works, the reappearance of the grand independent adagio in Op. 106—this fundamental deviation from the style of construction in the former group with its compact precise forms, might lead it to be supposed that these did not fulfil Beethoven's intentions, and that he was conscious of a certain discrepancy. But the extension of fixed forms does not lead us to expect their total abandonment. Besides Beethoven returns to the two-movement form in Op. 111, and the different movements of the last five works, with the exception, perhaps, of Op. 106, show no signs of an uniform plan throughout. One must also bear in mind that usages and proprieties could no longer exercise authority over the now independent Beethoven. He adhered to settled forms in so far only as they served as a means for the ideal expression he had in view. This was most clearly apparent in his last quartets, in which he drew all available artistic forms into his creative circle, regardless as to whether he had used them before or not. In his Symphonies, with the exception of the last ones, Beethoven never departed from the customary form, wisely reflecting that the universality for which such works are destined only accustoms itself very slowly to anything new. The sonata and quartet gave him better scope; for works of this class, on account of their limited musical material and the absence of the multiform tone-colouring of the great orchestra, require, for their appreciation a deeper and more cultivated musical sympathy and imagination.

Marx, in his " Music of the 19th century and Beethoven," has formed another classification of the Sonatas, founded on his views of the nature of music. Music, according to Marx, is threefold: mere tone-play, language of feeling (music of the soul), and music of the mind and spirit (ideal representation), the latter being found in the highest degree and almost exclusively with Beethoven. There is much to be said for this classification, especially if, like Marx, we do not draw a hard and fast line between the sections. Music is, and remains, pre-eminently an art of the emotional fancy; feeling, the music of the soul, is the ideal centre; and it appears as such even in tone-play—otherwise Hanslick would be right in saying that music was only a sounding arabesque. Feeling pervades also music of the mind— the ideal representation—for how else could intellect and ideal representation find any expression in sounds, if feeling were not the connecting medium? This classification can only be followed entirely in so far as a particular feature is the leading one in any particular work. Marx classifies thus:—

Mere Tone-Play.

Op. 2, No. 3; Op. 10, Nos. 1 and 2; Op. 14; Op. 22; Op. 27; Op. 31, Nos. 1 and 3; Op. 53; Op. 54; Op. 78; Op. 106.

Emotional Life.

Op. 2, Nos. 1 and 2; Op. 7; Op. 10, No. 3; Op. 13; Op. 26; Op. 28; Op. 31, No. 2; Op. 90.

Ideal Representation.

Op. 27, No. 2; Op. 57; Op. 81; Op. 101; Op. 109; Op. 110; Op. 111.

This grouping evinces, as indeed we need not to be told, that Marx had a deep insight into the meaning and spirit of the Sonatas. On some points, however, there will be considerable difference of opinion; the place given to the Sonata, Op. 106, will doubtless be especially criticised. Marx begins with the assertion that although none of the Sonatas in the sphere of pure tone-play are without a deeper meaning for the soul, yet they require technical capacity, first of all, and with it that "feeling" which comes instinctively to musically gifted and skilful performers. As if Op. 57, Op. 101, &c., did not also require technical capacity, and as if in Op. 106, mere "feeling" would be any more use to us than in any other works. That Op. 106 belongs to the third group appears to me incontrovertible. I think also that in the Sonatas, Op. 10, Nos. 1 and 2, Op. 22, Op. 27, No. 1, considered as a whole, not tone-play, but music of the soul predominates; again, Op. 31, No. 2, rises to ideal representation, which Marx also suggests as "perhaps demonstrable." Op. 6, Op. 49 and Op. 79, belong to the first group as a matter of course.

A classification of Beethoven's Sonatas according to the keys and the tempi is not without interest. The works, Op. 6, Op. 49, Op. 79 may reasonably be passed over here; on the other hand, the so-called trios, when they are in different keys to the minuet and scherzo, also the important intermediary movements, like the arioso in Op. 110, may be reckoned separately. Hence the following result :—

A. Tempi.

25 movements are in $\frac{2}{4}$ time.
24 ,, ,, $\frac{3}{4}$,,
26 ,, ,, $\frac{4}{4}$,,
3 ,, ,, $\frac{3}{8}$,,
10 ,, ,, $\frac{6}{8}$,,
2 ,, ,, $\frac{9}{8}$,,
1 movement is $\frac{12}{8}$,,
1 ,, ,, $\frac{9}{16}$,,
1 ,, ,, $\frac{12}{16}$,,

In addition to this $\frac{9}{16}$ and $\frac{12}{32}$ time appear in the Sonata, Op. 111, which alone has $\frac{9}{16}$ time, as Op. 57 has $\frac{12}{8}$, and Op. 110 has $\frac{12}{16}$ time.

B. Keys.

11 movements are in C major.
7 ,, ,, C minor.
2 ,, ,, C sharp major.
5 ,, ,, D flat major.
7 ,, ,, D major.
4 ,, ,, D minor.
12 ,, ,, E flat major.
2 ,, ,, E flat minor.
6 ,, ,, E major.
3 ,, ,, E minor.
9 ,, ,, F major.
7 ,, ,, F minor.
2 ,, ,, F sharp major.
1 movement is in F sharp minor.
5 movements are in G major.
2 ,, ,, G minor.
9 ,, ,, A flat major.
1 movement is in A flat minor.
7 movements are in B flat major.
2 ,, ,, B flat minor.

The favourite keys of the great masters are sometimes spoken of, and C minor has been particularly named as Beethoven's favourite key. The Sonatas do not confirm this; for in them C major, E flat major, F major, A flat major stand foremost. The idea that every key has something characteristic, and is specially adapted for the expression of certain states of mind and feeling, has been widely opposed, among others, by leading musical connoisseurs, for example, by Hauptmann ("Natur der Harmonik und Metrik.") It is contended that in every key there exist the same relations between the intervals, and the pitch gradually becomes higher with time; C major, the fundamental key, is higher now than it was a hundred years ago; consequently this key theory is pure self-deception, and the transposition of a piece of music into another key cannot alter the character of it. According to Schindler, Beethoven believed in the characteristic qualities of the different keys. Schindler says (Biography ii., 156, 3rd edition): "The opinions put forth by Beethoven were based on a thorough knowledge of every key. The pitch may move a whole tone higher or lower than the ear is accustomed to hear, but this has nothing to do with transposition and cuts away the ground from that argument, for the central point in the musical system must be in an immovable position; the pitch of the orchestra has imperceptibly become higher;

in like manner, also, our feeling for the 'psyche' of the keys, which must have its place in the scale of every key—a fact which the ancients duly recognized; but transposition is a sudden variation of at least half a tone, by which the feeling is suddenly removed into another sphere, because the 'psyche' is violently forced out of the first combination of sounds into another. If, therefore, there were no difficulty in distinguishing C sharp major from the enharmonic D flat major, the ear would be directed into a second line; there would be the sense of the subtle difference between hard and soft, and then the characteristic signs of both these keys." So far Beethoven briefly and to the point. It may be, then, most confidently stated that he was not governed by mere caprice in the choice of keys, but by the idea of the work and the nature of the particular movement. Can one imagine such characteristic works as the C sharp minor Sonata, the F minor Sonata, Op. 57, the C minor sonata, Op. 111, in other keys? Would not the traits of character which these works unfold to us become quite obliterated, and the pictures colourless? But I only wish to throw out a suggestion with regard to other points of view in which the sonatas may still be considered.

A comparison of Beethoven's Sonatas with his quartets and symphonies will lead the impartial observer to this among other conclusions, that as regards the working out of the several works, and the union and arrangement of the different movements, Beethoven, if we may use the expression, sometimes took things more easily in his sonatas than in his quartets and symphonies. Kullak says that Beethoven's weakness lies in the inequality of the style of a great number of his works. This is obviously saying too much, and does not touch the later Beethoven. But it may apply indeed to the Haydn-Mozart period of the master, when, as was shown in the discussion of the Sonatas in the former part, Beethoven now and then loses his cue. The heel of Achilles, in a great number of the Beethoven Sonatas, is to be found in the minuets, which indeed might just as well have been omitted, without interfering with the general configuration of the Sonata, for they seem to exist only because the four-movement form happened to be in vogue then. This is also directly confirmed by Beethoven himself. To wit, Schindler relates (Part II, page 215) that on the occasion of a proposed collective edition of the Sonatas, in which the poetical idea underlying each was to be set forth,

Beethoven considered whether it would not tend to the attainment of greater unity, if some of the four-movement Sonatas written at an earlier period when the four-movement form was the only one in accepted usage, were to be changed into the three-movement form. The sonatas, Op. 2, Nos. 2 and 3, Op. 22, Op. 26, Op. 28, Op. 31, No. 3, and according to our ideas, Op. 27, No. 2 could certainly dispense with their minuets without disadvantage. To this we might further add that, as it seems to me, in a great number of the minuets or scherzi, the middle movement, the so-called trio, or minor, is in a remarkable manner, the most original or at least the most characteristic part of the movement. I refer only to Op. 2, No. 3, Op. 7, Op. 10. No. 3, Op. 22, Op. 26, Op. 27, Op. 31, No. 3.

The study of Beethoven's Sonatas is no easy one, whether we consider them on their intellectual or their technical side. As he took his starting point from Haydn and Mozart, it seems quite necessary that we should not begin with him, but with his predecessors, for with Beethoven we come to the final point, "the entrance into the ideal" (Marx). Marx has provided a capital help in his "Appendix" to the Biography of Beethoven, and also in his work, "Guide to the Performance of Beethoven's Pianoforte Music." Both cannot be too warmly commended to the lovers of Beethoven, although I must content myself with thus referring to them. But it should be mentioned that as regards the technique, Marx gives the following gradation: Op. 6, Op. 49, Op. 79, Op. 14, Op. 13, Op. 2, Op. 10, Op. 22, Op. 26, Op. 28, Op. 7, Op. 54, Op. 31, Op. 90, Op. 27, Op. 81, Op. 101, Op. 110, Op. 57, Op. 109, Op. 53, Op. 111, Op. 106. With respect to the intellectual comprehension, the progress from the simple to the complex, he gives this order: Op. 2, Op. 13, Op. 14, Op. 22, Op. 54, Op. 53, Op. 78 (Op. 26, Op. 10, Op. 7, Op. 28, Op. 31, Op. 27, Op. 57), Op. 81, Op. 90, Op. 106, Op. 101, Op. 110, Op. 109, Op. 111. This arrangement, however, takes no heed of the very diversified character of Op. 2, Op. 14, Op. 10, Op. 31, Op. 27. Without subjective comprehension, and power of imagination no great musical work can be comprehended, not to speak of a Beethoven creation.

Beethoven's Sonatas have appeared in various editions. Among the best and cheapest is Hallberger's, of Stuttgart, the edition being uniform with that of Haydn and Mozart's Sonatas. Louis Köhler, of Königsberg, has recently* undertaken a duet arrangement of the Beethoven Sonatas. They are beautifully got up and published at a very moderate price by Henry Litolff (Brunswick). The edition includes also the Sonatas for the pianoforte, with accompaniments for the violin, 'cello, &c. Köhler has ably accomplished the task, and so well silenced any objections we might raise against the four-hand arrangement, that we cannot but agree with the reason which he gives in justification of his undertaking: that this duet-edition is especially adapted to the requirements of less technically accomplished players, for only by these means can the approach to the profoundest Sonatas be facilitated, since these also offer the greatest technical difficulties.

Thus will the Beethoven music extend into an ever-widening circle, the number of Beethoven's friends will increase from year to year, and the temple of true musical beauty will be more widely opened and become a greater blessing to mankind.

FINIS.

---

* 1866 [Translator].

Musical Books for Students.

ON CONDUCTING, a Treatise on Style in the Execution of Classical Music by R. Wagner, translated by E. Dannreuther, *Second Edition*, cr. 8vo, cloth, 5s.

MUSICAL DIRECTORY OF GREAT BRITAIN AND IRELAND, Professional and Trade, cr. 8vo, paper, 2s. (cloth, 3s. 6d.)

DELIVERY IN THE ART OF PIANOFORTE PLAYING, on Rhythm, Measure, Phrasing, Tempo by C. A. Ehrenfechter, cr. 8vo, cloth, 2s.

BIOGRAPHICAL DICTIONARY OF FIDDLERS, including performers on the Violoncello and Double Bass, past and present, containing a Sketch of their Artistic Career together with Notes of their Compositions by A. Mason Clarke, 9 portraits, post 8vo, cloth, 5s.

CHOPIN'S GREATER WORKS (Preludes, Ballads, Nocturnes, Polonaises, Mazurkas), How they should be understood by J. Kleczynski, including Chopin's Notes for a Method of of Methods, translated with additions by N. Janotha, with 3 portraits and facsimile, cr. 8vo, cloth, 5s.

TECHNICAL STUDY IN THE ART OF PIANOFORTE PLAYING (Deppe's Method), by C. A. Ehrenfecter, 3rd Edition, cr. 8vo, cloth, 2s. 6d.

BAPTIE (D.), Sketches of English Glee Composers, Historical, Biographical, and Critical, with Alphabetical Index of Composers and Chronological Index, as well as particulars of Prize Glees, 1763-1866, 2 portraits, post 8vo, bevelled cloth, 5s.
   This Work was Highly Commended by the "Church Times."

50 MUSICAL HINTS TO CLERGYMEN, Management of Breath, Classification of Male Voices, Management of the Voice, The Service, with twenty specially written Exercises by Geo. F. Grover, 1s.

CATECHISM OF PART SINGING AND THE CHORAL SERVICE. By John Hiles, 3rd Edition, thick post 8vo, price 1s.
   Advice to Singers on every point of interest in reference to the Vocal Organs.

THE THROAT IN ITS RELATION TO SINGING, a series of Popular Papers, by Whitfield Ward, A.M., M.D. *With engravings*, cloth, 3s. 6d.

HOW TO SING AN ENGLISH BALLAD. By E. Philp, 7th Edition, 6d.

VOCAL EXERCISES FOR CHOIRS AND SCHOOLS. By Dr. Westbrook, 2d.

WILLIAM REEVES, 185, Fleet Street, London, E.C.

Musical Books for Students.

COUNTERPOINT, a Simple and Intelligible Treatise containing the most important Rules of all Text Books in Catechetical form, for Beginners by A. L. Hirst, F.R.C.O. 9d.

RUDIMENTS OF VOCAL MUSIC. With 42 Preparatory Exercises, Rounds and Songs in the Treble Clef, by T. Mee Pattison, 2nd Edition, 4d.

SCHOOL BOARD SINGING TUTOR. By Dr. A. S. Holloway, 2d.

SOME FAMOUS SONGS, an Art Historical Sketch. By F. R. Ritter. 1s.

ELEMENTARY MUSIC, a Book for Beginners, with Questions and Vocal Exercises, by Dr. Westbrook, 12th Edition, 1s. (cloth, 1s. 6d.)

REEVES' MUSIC PRIMERS.

- TRANSPOSITION AT SIGHT, for Students of the Organ and Pianoforte. By H. Ernest Nichol, Mus. Bac. Oxon., *Second Edition*, 1s. (or cloth, 1s. 6d.)
- DUDLEY BUCK's New and Complete Pronouncing Dictionary of Musical Terms, 6d. (or cloth 1s.)
- ELEMENTARY MUSIC, 1s. (cloth, 1s. 6d.) By Dr. Westbrook.
- EXERCISES ON GENERAL ELEMENTARY MUSIC, a Book for Beginners. Part I., 9d. K. Paige.
- *Ditto*, Part II., 1s. [2 parts complete in cloth, 2s. 4d.]
- LIFE AND WORKS OF MOZART, 1s. (cloth, 1s. 6d.) Alfred Whittingham.
- LIFE AND WORKS OF HANDEL, 1s. (cloth, 1s. 6d.) Alfred Whittingham.

MODERN CHURCH MUSIC.

1—Easter Anthem, "Jesus Lives!" by Rev. T. Herbert Spinney, price 2d.
2—Anthem for Whitsuntide and General Use, "Come Holy Ghost our Souls Inspire," by Thomas Adams, F.R.C.O., price 2d.
3—Story of the Ascension by Rev. John Napleton, 1½d.
4—Anthem, "God so Loved the World," by J. Jamouneau, price 2d.
5—Magnificat in B flat, by Thomas Adams, F.R.C.O., 3d.
6—Nunc Dimittis in B flat, by Thos. Adams, F.R.C.O., 2d.
7—Four Kyries, by Charles Steggall, Berthold Tours, E. J. Hopkins, J. M. W. Young, price 1½d.
8—Te Deum, by T. E. Spinney, 1½d.
9—Anthem, "I Am the Good Shepherd," by G. Rayleigh Vicars, 2d.
10—Story of the Cross, Music by H. Clifton Bowker, 2d.

WILLIAM REEVES, 185, Fleet Street, London, E.C.

CATALOGUE OF PUBLICATIONS

Issued by **WILLIAM REEVES**,

LITERARY, ART AND MUSIC.

ALSO

WORKS ON FREEMASONRY.

Published and Sold by
WILLIAM REEVES, 83, CHARING CROSS ROAD, W.C.

THE o:——— WEEKLY ONE PENNY (or if with Supplement 2d.
(One week after date always 2d).

"MUSICAL STANDARD,"

A NEWSPAPER FOR MUSICIANS, - - - -
PROFESSIONAL AND AMATEUR.

Gives Supplements of Illustrations of British and Foreign Organs, Portraits of Eminent Musicians, Organ Music, Violin Music, Anthems, Part Songs, etc.

Yearly subscription 7s. 6d., abroad, 9s. 9d., post free.

Illustrated Series, Vols. 1, 2, 3, 4, 5, 6, 7, 8, 9 & 10 bound in brown cloth, 5s. each.

Handsome Covers for Binding, 1s. 6d. each, (by post 1s. 9d).

Publishing and Advertising Offices:
83, CHARING CROSS ROAD, LONDON, W.C.

Paper, 2s.: or Cloth, 3s. 6d.

MUSICAL DIRECTORY

FOR GREAT BRITAIN AND IRELAND.

THE TRADES, PROFESSORS AND OTHERS CONNECTED WITH MUSIC, CHORAL SOCIETIES, STAFF OF CATHEDRALS, COLLEGES AND ABBEY CHURCHES, ETC.

W. REEVES, 83, CHARING CROSS ROAD, LONDON, W.C.

THE ORGANIST'S QUARTERLY JOURNAL

Of Original Compositions.

FOUNDED BY DR. WILLIAM SPARK
City Organist, Leeds.

New Series VOLUMES I. & II., containing 160 large pages bound in cloth, 18s. each.

For list of the Contents of the Parts. *See pages 16 & 17*

W. REEVES, 83, CHARING CROSS ROAD, W.C.

The Violin Times, Monthly, 2d., (by post 2½d.)

Edited by E. POLONASKI.

Subscription, 2s. 6d., per Year, - Abroad, 3s.
VOLS. 1 TO 5, BOUND, PRICE 6/- EACH.   Covers for binding 2s. each.

LARGE EDITION, over 1,000 pp., imp. 8vo.

CHAFFERS (W^m.), MARKS AND MONOGRAMS ON EUROPEAN AND ORIENTAL POTTERY AND PORCELAIN, with Historical Notices of each Manufactory, preceded by an Introductory Essay on Ancient Pottery and on the Vasa Fictilia of England and Mediæval Earthenware Vessels, with over 3,500 Potters Marks and Illustrations, revised and edited by F. Litchfield, ornamental cloth, Ninth Edition, with Additional Information and Marks, 42s.

EIGHTH EDITION, CONSIDERABLY AUGMENTED AND CAREFULLY REVISED BY A. MARKHAM.

CHAFFERS (W.), HALL MARKS ON GOLD AND SILVER PLATE, Illustrated with Revised Tables of Annual Date Letters employed in the Assay Offices of the United Kingdom, 346 pp., roy. 8vo, cloth, 16s.

This edition contains a History of the Goldsmith's Trade in France, with extracts from the decrees relating thereto, and engravings of the standard and other Marks used in that country as well as in other foreign States. The Provincial Tables of England and Scotland contain many hitherto unpublished Marks; all the recent enactments are quoted. The London Tables (which have never been surpassed for correctness) may now be considered complete. Many valuable Hints to Collectors are given, and cases of fraud alluded to, etc.

CHAFFERS W.), COLLECTOR'S HANDBOOK OF MARKS AND MONOGRAMS ON POTTERY AND PORCELAIN OF THE RENAISSANCE AND MODERN PERIOD, selected from his larger work, New Edition Revised and considerably Augmented by F. Litchfield, Twelfth Thousand, 234 pp., post 8vo, cloth, gilt, 6s.

THE COMPANION TO "HALL MARKS ON GOLD AND SILVER PLATE."

CHAFFERS (W.), GILDA AURIFABRORUM, A History of English Goldsmiths and Plateworkers and their Marks stamped on Plate, copied in *facsimile* from celebrated Examples and the earliest Records preserved at Goldsmiths' Hall, London, with their names, addresses and dates of entry, 2,500 *Illustrations;* also Historical Account of the Goldsmiths' Company and their Hall Marks and Regalia; the Mint; Closing of the Exchequer; Goldsmith Banks, Shop Signs, a Copious Index, etc., a New Edition, 267 pp., roy. 8vo, cloth, 12s.

CHAFFERS (Wm.) HANDBOOK TO HALL MARKS ON GOLD AND SILVER PLATE, with Revised Tables of Annual Date Letters Employed in the Assay Offices of England, Scotland and Ireland, Edited and Extended by C. A. Markham., *F.S.A.*, cr. 8vo, cloth, 5s.

MARKHAM (C.), HANDBOOK TO FRENCH HALL MARKS ON GOLD AND SILVER PLATE. Illustrated. Crown 8vo, cloth, 5s.   1900

The above 2 works, in conjunction with CHAFFERS' HANDBOOK complete the set of HANDBOOKS.

MARKHAM (Chr. A., *F.S.A.*). HANDBOOK TO FOREIGN HALL MARKS ON GOLD AND SILVER PLATE (except those on French Plate), containing 163 stamps, cr. 8vo, cloth, 5s.

COBBETT (W.), RURAL RIDES in the Counties of Surrey, Kent, Sussex, Hants., Wilts., Gloucestershire, etc., edited with Life, New Notes, and the addition of a copious Index, New Edition by PITT COBBETT, *map and portrait*, 2 vols, cr. 8vo, xlviii. and 806 pp.), cloth gilt, 12s. 6d.

Cobbett's "Rural Rides" is to us a delightful book, but it is one which few people know. We are not sure that up to the present time it was impossible to get a nice edition of it: We are therefore glad to see that Messrs: Reeves & Turner's recently published edition is a very creditable production, two handy well-filled volumes.—*Gardening.*

KEATS (John), THE POETICAL WORKS OF JOHN KEATS (large type), given from his own Editions and other Authentic Sources, and collated with many Manuscripts, edited by H. Buxton Forman, *portrait*, SIXTH EDITION,   8 pp., cr. 8vo, buckram, 8s.

LONG (W. H.), A DICTIONARY OF THE ISLE OF WIGHT DIALECT, and of Provincialisms used in the Island, with Illustrative Anecdotes and Tales, etc.,

Songs sung by the Peasantry, forming a Treasury of Island Manners and Customs Fifty Years Ago, 182 pp., post 8vo, cloth, 2s. 6d.

MALTHUS (T. R.), AN ESSAY ON THE PRINCIPLE OF POPULATION, or a View of its Past and Present Effects on Human Happiness, with an Inquiry into our Prospect respecting the Future Removal or Mitigation of the Evils which it Occasions, Ninth Edition, 567 pp., 8vo, cloth, 8s.

SHELLEY LIBRARY (The), An Essay in Bibliography, by H. Buxton Forman, Shelley's Books, Pamphlets and Broadsides, Posthumous Separate Issues, and Posthumous Books, wholly or mainly by him, 127 pp., 8vo, part 1, wrappers, 3s. 6d.

SHELLEY (Percy Bysshe), THE POETICAL WORKS OF (in large type), given from his own Editions and other Authentic Sources, collated with many MSS., and with all Editions of Authority, together with his Prefaces and Notes, his Poetical Translations and Fragments, and an Appendix of Juvenalia, Edited by H. Buxton Forman, Third Edition, with the Notes of Mary Wollstonecraft Shelley, *fine etched portrait*, 2 vols., cr. 8vo, cloth (with Design in Gold on cover by Rossetti), 12s.

SIDONIA THE SORCERESS, by William Meinhold, Translated by Lady Wilde, with the Amber Witch, translated by Lady Duff Gordon, in 2 vols., crown 8vo, 8s. 6d.   1894

THOMSON (James "B V."), POETICAL WORKS, The City of Dreadful Night, Vane's Story, Weddah and Om-el-Bonain, Voice from the Hell, and Poetical Remains, Edited by B. Dobell, with Memoir and Portrait, 2 vols, thick cr. 8vo, cloth, 12s. 6d.

THOMSON (James, "B. V."), BIOGRAPHICAL AND CRITICAL STUDIES, 483 pages, cr. 8vo, cloth, 6s.

HISTORICAL, BIOGRAPHICAL WORKS, &c.

MAKERS OF MUSIC, Biographical Sketches of the Great Composers, With Chronological Summaries of their Works, and Facsimiles from Musical MSS. of Bach, Handel, Purcell, Dr. Arne, Gluck, Haydn, Mozart, Beethoven, Weber, Schubert, Berlioz, Mendelssohn, Chopin, Schumann, Wagner, Verdi, Gounod, Brahms, and Grieg, With General Chronological Table, By R. Farquharson Sharp, Portrait of Henry Purcell, cr. 8vo. cloth, 5s.

HOW TO MANAGE A CHORAL SOCIETY. By N. Kilburn, 2nd Edition, post 8vo., 6d.

WAGNER'S PARSIFAL and the Bayreuth Fest-Spielhaus. By N. Kilburn, cr. 8vo., 6d.

WAGNER, A Sketch of his Life and Works, by N. Kilburn, 6d.

WOMAN AS A MUSICIAN, an art Historical Study by F. R. Ritter, 8vo., 1s.

ÆSTHETICS OF MUSICAL ART, or the Beautiful in Music by Dr. F. Hand, translated by W. E. Lawson, Mus. Bac., cr. 8vo., cloth, 5s.

EHLERT (Louis), Letters on Music to a Lady, translated by F. Raymond Ritter, cr. 8vo., bevelled cloth, gilt edges, 4s. 6d., plain cl. 4s.

CHERUBINI, Memorials illustrative of his Life, by E. Bellasis, thick crown 8vo., cloth, 6s.

FRANZ LISZT, ARTIST AND MAN, 1811-1840, by L. Ramann, trans. by E. Cowdery, 2 vols., thick cr. 8vo., 10s. 6d. (pub. 24s.) (covers faded).

BERLIOZ, LIFE AND LETTERS, from the French by H. M. Dunstan, 2 vols., cr. 8vo., cloth, 7s. 6d. (pub. 21s.) (covers not quite fresh).

JOHANNES BRAHMS, A Biographical Sketch, translated with additions by Rosa Newmarch, edited with preface by J. A. Fuller Maitland, cr. 8vo., cl., 2s. 6d. (pub. 6s.)

THE BACH LETTERS. Letters of Samuel Wesley, relating to the Introduction into England of the Works of J. S. Bach. Edited by E. Wesley. 2nd Edition, 8vo. cloth, 2s. 6d.

CHOPIN (F.), His Life, Letters and Works, by M. Karasowski, trans. by E. Hill, *Portrait*, 2 vols, 8vo. cloth, 12s. 6d.

BALFE, His Life and Works, by W. A. Barrett, cr. 8vo, bevelled cloth, 3s. 6d. (pub. 7s. 6d.)

FREDERIC FRANCOIS CHOPIN, by Charles Willeby, with engraved portrait, cr. 8vo, cloth, 3s. 6d. (pub. 10s. 6d.)

STATHAM (H. H.), Form and Design in Music, a Brief Outline of the Æsthetic conditions of the Art, addressed to general Readers (in a readable Literary form . . . in everyday language), 8vo, cloth, 2s. (pub. 5s.)

BEETHOVEN, by Richard Wagner, with a Supplement from the Philosophical Works of Arthur Schopenhauer, translated by Edward Dannreuther, Second Ed., cr. 8vo, cloth, 6s.

CHOPIN, LIFE OF, by Franz Liszt, new and very much Enlarged Edition, cr. 8vo, cloth, *Ready in Autumn of* 1899.

WAGNER, Der Ring des Nibelungen, Being the Story concisely told of Das Rhinegold, Die Walküre, Siegfried and Götterdämmerung, by N. Kilburn, post 8vo, 9d.

RICHARD WAGNER's Letters to his Dresden Friends, Theodor Uhlig, Wilhelm Fischer and Ferdinand Heine, translated with a preface by J. S. Shedlock and an etching of Wagner by C. W. Sherborn, thick cr. 8vo, cloth, gilt top, 6s. 6d. (pub. 12s. 6d.)

Box (C.), Church Music in the Metropolis, its Past and Present Condition, with Notes Critical and Explanatory, post 8vo, cloth, 3s. (covers a bit soiled).

THE PAST AND THE FUTURE, INAUGRAL LECTURE AT GRESHAM COLLEGE, Nov. 1890, by J. Frederick Bridge, Mus. Doc., cr. 8vo, sewed, 6d.

ENGLISH HYMN TUNES from the 16th Century to the Present Time, by the Rev. A. W. Malim, containing 21 Musical Illustrations, 8vo, sewed, 1s.

BEETHOVEN, Life of, by Louis Nohl, translated by John J. Lalor, 2nd Edition, cr. 8vo, bevelled cloth, **gilt edges, 3s. 6d**

BEETHOVEN, Reminiscences of the artistic and Home Life of the Artist, from the diary of a Lady in close personal intercourse with him, by L. Nohl, translated by A. Wood, 8vo, cloth, 3s. 6d. (pub. 10s. 6d.)

BEETHOVEN DEPICTED BY HIS CONTEMPORARIES, by Ludwig Nohl, translated by E. Hill, 2nd Edition, thick cr. 8vo, cloth, 7s. 6d.

EDUCATIONAL.

DICTIONARY OF MUSICIANS, New and Enlarged Edition brought completely up to date, post 8vo, sewed, 1s. cloth, 1s. 6d.

MUSIC, A First Book for Beginners embodying the most recent English and Continental Teaching by a Professor [Alfred Whittingham], post 8vo, 4d.

The two principal objects kept in view in writing this little book were Thoroughness of Definition and Regular Order in the arrangement of Subjects. It differs from all other similar Works in that all the Technical Terms in Music are introduced in the Answers not in the Questions.

COUNTERPOINT: A Simple and Intelligible Treatise, Containing the most Important Rules of all Text Books, in Catechetical Form; (Forming an Answer to the Question "What is Counterpoint?") Intended for Beginners. By A. Livingstone Hirst, cr. 8vo, sewed, 9d.

MANUAL OF MUSICAL HISTORY, from the Epoch of Ancient Greece to our present time by Dr. F. L. Ritter, 2nd Edition, cr. 8vo, cl., 2s. 6d.

ON CONDUCTING, by Richard Wagner, translated by E. Dannreuther, Second Edition, cr. 8vo., cloth, 5s.

MUSIC IN AMERICA, by Dr. F. L. Ritter, cr. 8vo bevelled cloth, 7s. 6d.

DUDLEY BUCK'S Complete Pronouncing Dictionary of Musical Terms. By Dr. Dudley Buck. *New Edition with the Pronunciation of each Term accurately given,* **cr. 8vo, paper cover 6d. (cloth 1s).**

A Correct Pronouncing Dictionary of all the Terms used in Music has not yet been Published in England, though the importance of such a work for use in Schools can hardly be over estimated. A pupil going home from School with incorrect and imperfect pronunciation of Technical Terms compares unfavourably with another pupil from another school whose pronunciation is correct. The Correct Pronunciation of Musical Terms is a very simple matter, and being easily taught, and easily learned, there can be no excuse for its neglect.

THE STUDENT'S HELMHOLTZ, Musical Acoustics or the Phenomena of Sound as connected with Music, by

John Broadhouse, with more than 100 Illustrations, 3rd Edition, cr. 8vo, cloth, 7s. 6d.

THE STUDENT'S HISTORY OF MUSIC. History of Music, from the Christian Era to the present time by Dr. F. L. Ritter. 3rd Edition, thick cr. 8vo., cloth, 7s. 6d.

ELEMENTARY MUSIC. A book for Beginners, by Dr. Westbrook, with Questions and Vocal Exercises, Twelfth Edition, 1s., (cloth, 1s. 6d).

PURITY IN MUSIC, by A. F. Thibaut. Translated by J. Broadhouse. Schumann says: "A fine book about music, read it frequently." Crown 8vo., cloth, 2s. 6d.

LIFE AND WORKS OF HANDEL. By A. Whittingham. 1s. (cloth, 1s. 6d.)

LIFE AND WORKS OF MOZART. By A. Whittingham. 1s. (cloth, 1s. 6d.)

EXERCISES ON GENERAL ELEMENTARY MUSIC. A Book for Beginners, by K. Paige, 4th Edition, Part I. price 9d., Part II. price 1s. (2 parts complete in cloth, 2/4
The *Musical Times* speaks in the highest terms of this work.

DR. AHN'S FIRST FRENCH COURSE. Edited by S. Bartlett (Head Master Mercers' and Stationers' School), Post 8vo., cloth 1s. 6d.

WORKS ON THE PIANOFORTE, &c.

GREATER WORKS OF CHOPIN, (Polonaises, Mazurkas, Nocturnes, etc.) and how they should be played, by J. Kleczynski, translated by Miss N. Janotha and edited by Sutherland Edwards, with Portrait, Facsimile, etc., cr. 8vo, cloth, 5s.

MUSIC AND MUSICIANS, Essays and Criticisms, by Robert Schumann, translated, edited and annotated by F. R. Ritter, Portrait of Robert Schumann, photographed from a Crayon by Bendemann, First Series, Fourth Edition, thick cr. 8vo, cloth, 8s. 6d.

Ditto, Second Series, Second Edition, thick cr. 8vo, cloth, 10s. 6d.

EHRENFECHTER (C. A.), Technical Study in the art of Pianoforte Playing (Deppe's principles), with numerous illustrations, third edition, cr. 8vo, bevelled cloth, 2s. 6d

EHRENFECHTER (C. A.), Delivery in the Art of Pianoforte Playing, on Rhythm, Measure, Phrasing, Tempo, cr. 8vo, cloth, 2s.

BEETHOVEN'S PIANOFORTE SONATAS Explained by Ernst von Elterlein trans. by E. Hill, with Preface by Ernst Pauer, Entirely new and revised edition (the Fifth), with Portrait, Facsimile and View of House, cr. 8vo. cl., 3s. 6d.

BEETHOVEN'S SYMPHONIES in their Ideal Significance, explained by Ernst von Elterlein, translated by Francis Weber, with an account of the facts relating to Beethoven's 10th Symphony, by L. Nohl, *Second Edition*, with Portrait, cr. 8vo, cloth, 3s. 6d.

BEETHOVEN'S SYMPHONIES Critically discussed by A. T. Teetgen. *Second Edition*, cloth, 3s. 6d.

THE DEPPE FINGER EXERCISES for rapidly developing an Artistic Touch in Pianoforte playing, carefully arranged, classified and explained by Amy Fay, English Fingering, folio, 1s. 6d. (Continental Fingering, 1s. 6d.)

HOW TO PLAY CHOPIN. The Works of Chopin and their proper Interpretation. By KLECZYNSKI, translated by A. WHITTINGHAM. 3rd Ed., *Woodcut & Music Illus.* post 8vo., cloth 3s. 6d.

PLAIDY'S PIANOFORTE TEACHER'S GUIDE. Translated by F. R. RITTER. Post 8vo., boards, 1s.

SCHUMANN'S RULES AND MAXIMS for Young Musicians. 4d.

PRACTICE REGISTER for Pupils Daily Practice. A specimen, 1d., or 1s. 4d. per 100.

REEVES' VAMPING TUTOR, Art of Extemporaneous Accompaniment or Playing by Ear on the Pianoforte, rapidly enabling anyone having an ear for music (with or without any knowledge of musical notation), to accompany Waltzes, Polkas, Songs, and with equal facility in any key, with practical examples, including Ma Normandi (in C) Lilla's a Lady, The Swiss Boy, Home Sweet Home, Blue Bells of Scotland, Nancy Dawson, Ma Normandie (in A), The Miller of the Dee, by Francis Taylor, folio, 2s.

The Great Classic for the Piano.

BACH (J. S.), 48 Preludes and 48 Fugues in all the major and minor keys, in 2 vols, folio, 3s. each (or in 1 vol, stiff covers, cloth back, 7s. 6d.

MOZART'S Don Giovanni, a Commentary, from the 3rd French Edition of Charles Gounod, by W. Clark and J. T. Hutchinson, cr. 8vo, cloth, 3s. 6d.

TUNING THE PIANOFORTE.—SMITH (Hermann), The Art of Tuning the Pianoforte, a New and Comprehensive Treatise to enable the musician to Tune his Pf. upon the System founded on the Theory of Equal Temperament, cr. 8vo, limp cloth, 2s.

Readers will welcome this note of approval signed A. J. Hipkins, a name long associated with the Pianoforte, and familiar to most musicians in the musical literature of the present time. No better voucher could be desired of the fair claims of this little book upon the readers' attention and confidence "I have had the privilege of reading the proofs of Mr. Hermann Smith's clear and exhaustive treatise on Pianoforte Tuning, and I am satisfied that for the professional tuner, or the amateur who desires to understand the subject and put the knowledge he acquires into practice, there is no book upon it yet published that may be compared with it. I recommend all tuners, or would-be tuners, to study this unpretending and excellent work, wherein the theory is laid down in clear and correct terms, and the practice, as far as this is possible is indicated judiciously."

THE VIOLIN.

INFORMATION FOR PLAYERS, OWNERS, DEALERS AND MAKERS OF BOW INSTRUMENTS, ALSO FOR STRING MANUFACTURERS, taken from Personal Experiences, Studies and Observations, by William Hepworth, with Illustrations of Stainer and Guarnerius Violins, etc., cr. 8vo, cloth, 2s. 6d.

NOTICE OF ANTHONY STRADIVARI, the celebrated Violin Maker known by the name of Stradivarius, preceded by Historical and Critical Researches on the Origin and Transformations of Bow Instruments, and followed by a Theoretical Analysis of the Bow, etc., by F. J. Fetis, translated by J. Bishop, Facsimile, 8vo, cloth, 5s.

BIOGRAPHICAL DICTIONARY OF FIDDLERS, including Performers on the Violoncello and Double Bass, Past and Present, containing a Sketch of their Artistic Career, together with Notes of their Compositions, by A. Mason Clarke, with 9 portraits, post 8vo, bevelled cl., 5s.

HOW TO MAKE A VIOLIN, Practically Treated, 2 Folding Plates and many Illustrations, by J. Broadhouse, cr. 8vo, bevelled cloth, 3s. 6d.

VIOLIN MANUFACTURE IN ITALY AND ITS GERMAN ORIGIN, by Dr. E. Schebek, translated by W. E. Lawson, 8vo., sewed, 1s.

SKETCHES OF GREAT VIOLINISTS AND GREAT PIANISTS, Biographical and Anecdotal, with Account of the Violin and Early Violinists (Viotti, Spohr, Paganini, De Beriot, Ole Bull, Clementi, Moscheles, Schumann (Robert and Clara), Chopin, Thalberg, Gottschalk, Liszt), by G. T. Ferris; *Second Edition*, bevelled cloth, 3s 6d. (or gilt edges 4s. 6d.)

FACTS ABOUT FIDDLES, Violins Old and New. By J. Broadhouse, 3rd Edition, 6d.

TECHNICS OF VIOLIN PLAYING. By KARL COURVOISIER. *With Illustrations*, 4th Edition, paper 1s. (or cloth, thick paper, 2s. 6d.) Highly commended by Joachim.

HOW TO PLAY THE FIDDLE, for Beginners on the Violin. By H. W. and G. Gresswell. 4th edition, 1s., (cl, 2s.)

AUTOBIOGRAPHY OF LOUIS SPOHR. 2 vols in 1, thick 8vo. cloth, 7s. 6d. (pub. 15s.)

TREATISE ON THE STRUCTURE AND PRESERVATION OF THE VIOLIN AND ALL OTHER BOW INSTRUMENTS, together with an account of the most celebrated makers and of the genuine characteristics of their Instruments, by J. A. Otto, with additions by J. Bishop, cr. 8vo, cloth, 3s.

WORKS ON THE ORGAN.

ANALYSIS OF MENDELSSOHN'S ORGAN WORKS, a Study of their Structural Features, for the use of Students, 127 Musical Examples, portrait and facsimiles cr. 8vo bevelled cloth, 4s. 6d

ORGANIST'S QUARTERLY JOURNAL of Original Compositions. Edited by Dr. W. Spark, non-subscribers, 5s. net, (yearly subscriptions, 10s. 6d., post free).

New Series Volumes I and II, 160 large pages, oblong folio, bound in cloth, 18s. each.

RINK'S PRACTICAL ORGAN SCHOOL: A New Edition, Carefully Revised. The Pedal Part printed on a separate Staff, and the Preface, Remarks and Technical Terms translated from the German, expressly for this edition by John Hiles. The Six Books Complete, handsomely bound in red cloth, gilt edges, ob. folio, 10s. 6d. (issued at 20s.), or the six parts 7s. 6d. (issued at 6s. each.)

A SHORT HISTORY OF THE ORGAN, Organists, and Services of the Chapel of Alleyn's College, Dulwich, with Extracts from the Diary of the Founder, by W. H Stocks, cr. 8vo, sewed, 1s.

THE INFLUENCE OF THE ORGAN IN HISTORY. By Dudley Buck, 1s.

HENRY SMART'S ORGAN COMPOSITIONS Analysed. By J. Broadhouse, cr. 8vo, cloth, 2s. 6d.

REFORM IN ORGAN BUILDING, by Thomas Casson, 6d.

THE ORGAN, Its Compass, Tablature, and Short and Incomplete Octaves, by John W. Warman, A.C.O. imp. 8vo, sewed, 3s. 6d. or boards, cloth back, 4s. 6d.

CATECHISM for the Harmonium and American Organ, by John Hiles, post 8vo, sewed, 1s.

RIMBAULT (Dr. E. F.), The Early English Organ Builders and their Works, from the 15th Century to the Period of the Great Rebellion, an unwritten chapter on the History of the Organ, Well printed, with woodcuts, post 8vo, cloth, 3s. 6d.

VOICE AND SINGING

TWELVE LESSONS ON BREATHING AND BREATH CONTROL, for Singers, Speakers and Teachers, by Geo. E. Thorp, crown 8vo, limp cloth, 1s.

TWENTY LESSONS ON THE DEVELOPMENT OF THE VOICE, or Singers, Speakers and Teachers, by Geo. E. Thorp, crown 8vo, imp cloth, 1s.

50 MUSICAL HINTS TO CLERGYMEN, Management of Breath, Classification of Male Voices, Management of the Voice, The Service, with twenty specially written Exercises by Geo. F. Grover, 1s.

CATECHISM OF PART SINGING AND THE CHORAL SERVICES. By John Hiles, 3rd Edition, thick post 8vo, price 1s.

Advice to Singers on every point of interest in reference to the Vocal Organs

THE THROAT IN ITS RELATION TO SINGING, a series of Popular Papers by Whitfield Ward, A.M., M.D. *With engravings*, cloth, 3s 6d.

HOW TO SING AN ENGLISH BALLAD. By E. Philp, 7th Edition, 6d.

VOCAL EXERCISES FOR CHOIRS AND SCHOOLS. By Dr. Westbrook, 2d.

RUDIMENTS OF VOCAL MUSIC. With 42 Preparatory Exercises, Rounds and Songs in the Treble Clef, by T. Mee Pattison, 2nd Ed., 4d.

SOME FAMOUS SONGS, an Art Historical Sketch. By F. R. Ritter. 1s.

MISCELLANEOUS.

LORD CHESTERFIELD'S LETTERS TO HIS SON.—Edited with Occasional Elucidatory Notes, Translations of all the Latin, French and Italian Quotations, and a Biographical Notice of the Author. By Chas. Stokes Carey, 2 vols, cr. 8vo, bevelled cloth, 10s. 6d.

FLAGELLATION AND THE FLAGELLANTS, A History of the Rod, in all Countries by the Rev. W. M. Cooper. *Plates and Cuts*, thick cr. 8vo, cloth, 7s. 6d. (published at 12s. 6d.)

CLASSICAL WORKS.
Edited by Prof. Anthon.

ANTHON'S HORACE, Edited by Rev. James Boyd, LL.D., thick post 8vo, 5s. 6d.

ANTHON'S HOMER'S ILIAD, First Three Books, Edited by B. Davies, LL.D., thick post 8vo, 5s 6d.

ANTHON'S CÆSAR'S COMMENTARIES, Edited by Rev. G. B. Wheeler thick post 8vo, 4s. 6d.

ANTHON'S VIRGIL, Edited by Rev. W. Trollope, M.A., thick post 8vo, 5s. 6d.

ANTHON'S ECLOGUES AND GEORGICS OF VIRGIL, with English Notes, Critical and Explanatory, and a Metrical Index, post 8vo, price 4s. 6d.

ANTHON'S SALLUST, Edited by Rev. J. Boyd. LL.D. post 8vo, 4s. 6d.

ANTHON'S JUVENAL AND PERSIUS' SATIRES, Edited by J. T. Wheeler, post 8vo, 4s. 6d.

ANTHON'S CICERO'S ORATIONS, with English Commentary and Historical, Geographical and Legal Indexes, Revised and Edited by Rev. G. B. Wheeler, post 8vo, 4s. 6d.

RUDIMENTS OF GREEK GRAMMAR, by E. Wettenhall, DD., translated by Rev. G. N. Wright, numerous annotations and Questions for Examination, by Rev. G. B. Wheeler, 3s.

NATIONAL SCHOOL OF OPERA IN ENGLAND; being The Substance of a Paper read before the Licentiates of Trinity College, March, 1882, by Frank Austin, post 8vo, sewed, 6d.

MUSICAL SHORTHAND for Composers, Students of Harmony Counterpoint, etc., can be written very rapidly and is more legible than printed music, with Specimen's from Bach, Handel, Chopin, Wagner, Mendelssohn, Spohr, Mozart, etc., by Francis Taylor, 14 pages, 12mo, 6d.

"Composers and Students of Music expend a vast amount of time in mere painful mechanism." We have only six totally unlike signs. These from their simplicity can be written with great rapidity, one dip of the pen sufficing for an entire page, and the writing being as legible as possible.—*Preface*.

HOW TO UNDERSTAND WAGNER'S "RING OF THE NIBELUNG," being the Story and a Descriptive Analysis of the "Rheingold," the "Valkyr," "Siegfried" and the "Dusk of the Gods," with a number of Musical Examples by Gustave Kobbé, Sixth Edition, post 8vo, cloth, 3s. 6d.

"To be appreciated in the smallest way Wagner must be studied in advance.—*Illustrated London News*.

RATIONAL ACCOMPANIMENT TO THE PSALMS by F. Gilber Webb, post 8vo, 6d.

HOW TO PLAY FROM SCORE.—Treatise on Accompaniment from Score on the Organ or Pianoforte, by

F. J. Fetis, trans. by A. Whittingham, cr. 8vo, cloth, 3s. 6d.

FRANZ LISZT, by T. Carlaw Martin, 6d. (No. 1 of St. Cecilia Biography Series).

LIFE OF ROBERT SCHUMANN, with Letters, 1833-1852, by von Wasielewski, Translated by A. L. Alger, with Preface by W. A. Barrett, B. Mus., cr. 8vo, cloth, 8s. 6d.

VOICE PRODUCTION AND VOWEL ENUNCIATION, by F. F. Mewburn Levien, Diagrams by Arthur C. Behrend, post 8vo, 6d.

"The most informing and interesting of all the Musical Journals."

THE MUSIC STUDENT.—A Scholastic Musical Monthly for Professor and Pupil, Devoted to the Violin Pianoforte, Singing, Harmony and Composition, Monthly 2d. (by post 2½d.), Annual Subscription, post free, 2s. 6d. (Abroad post free, 3s.)

CHOIR LISTS FOR SUNDAY SERVICES.

No. 1. Morning and Evening, printed in red, 1s. 4d. per 100.

No. 2. Morning, Afternoon, and Evening, printed in red, 1s. 6d. per 100.

No. 3. Morning and Evening, printed in red and black, 1s. 8d. per 100.

No. 4. Morning and Even., printed in red 1s. 4d. per 100.

No. 5. Quarto Size, Matins, Litany, Holy Communion, First Evensong, Second Evensong, Gothic Letter, printed in red, 6d. per dozen, 3s. per 100.

CHOIR ATTENDANCE REGISTER, 8vo, cloth.

No. 1. Ruled for a Choir of 20 or less, for one year, beginning at any date, 1s. 6d.

No. 2. Ruled for a Choir of 40 or less, for one year, beginning at any date, 2s.

No. 3. Ruled for a choir of 60 or less, for one year, beginning at any date, 2s. 6d.

NATIONAL AND PATRIOTIC SONG ALBUM, with Pf. Acc., containing the following popular pieces:—
A handsome Copyright Folio Volume of 81 pages, with coloured cover, printed on good paper, 2s. 6d.

(Formerly R. Cocks & Co.)

God Bless the Prince of Wales
Dear England
Victoria
God Bless our Sailor Prince
Here's a Health unto His Majesty
Lord of the Sea
The Roast Beef of Old England
The Blue Bells of Scotland
Tom Bowling
Come Lassies and Lads
Ye Mariners of England
The Bay of Biscay
Hearts of Oak
Stand United
The Cause of England's Greatness
The Last Rose of Summer
The Leather Bottle
Home Sweet Home
Three Cheers for the Red White and Blue
The Minstrel Boy
The British Grenadiers
Auld Lang Syne
Rule Britannia
God Save the Queen
Short Biographical Sketches

MODERN CHURCH MUSIC.
1. Easter Anthem, "Jesus Lives!" by Rev. T. Herbert Spinney, price 2d.
2. Anthem for Whitsuntide and General Use, "Come Holy Ghost our Souls Inspire," by Thomas Adams, F.R.C.O., price 2d.
3. Story of the Ascension, by Rev. John Napleton, price 1½d.
4. Anthem, "God so Loved the World," by J. Jamouneau, price 2d.
5. Magnificat in B flat, by Thomas Adams, F.R.C.O., Price 3d.
6. Nunc Dimittis in B flat, by Thomas Adams, F.R.C.O., Price 2d.
7. Four Kyries, by Charles Steggall, Berthold Tours, E. J. Hopkins, J. M. W. Young, price 1½d.
8. Te Deum, by T. E. Spinney, 1½d.
9. Anthem, "I am the Good Shepherd," by G. Rayleigh Vicars, 2d.
10. Story of the Cross, Music by H. Clifton Bowker, 2d.

POPULAR PART SONGS.
1. Merrily goes the Mill, by T. B. Southgate, 1d.
2. Take, O Take those Lips away, Part Song for S.A.T.B. by Claude E. Cover, A.R.C.O., 1½d.
3. Pack Clouds Away, for S.A.T.B.; by Claude E. Cover, A.R.C.O., 2d.

MARCHES, for the Pianoforte by John Philip Sousa, Folio Album, 1s., containing:—
1. The Washington Post.
2. Manhatton Beach.
3. The Liberty Bell.
4. High School Cadets.
5. The Belle of Chicago.
6. The Corcoran Cadets.
7. Our Flirtation.
8. March past of the Rifle Regiment.
9. March past of the National Fencibles.
10. Semper Fidelis.

Performing Edition.

THE CREATION, A Sacred Oratorio composed by Joseph Haydn, Vocal Score, The Pianoforte Accompaniment arranged and the whole edited by G. A. Macfarren, 8vo, paper covers, 2s., boards, 2s. 6d., scarlet cloth, 4s.

SIXTY YEARS OF MUSIC: A Record of the Art in England during the Victorian Era, containing 70 Portraits of the most Eminent Musicians, oblong quarto, boards, cloth back, 2s. 6d.

The Organist's Quarterly Journal

Of Original Compositions.

Founded by DR. Wm. SPARK, Late Organist, Town Hall, Leeds

Non-subscribers, 5/- each. Subscription, 10/6 for 4 issues.

New Series, Vol 1, containing 160 large pages, bound in cloth, 18s.

Part 12, New Series

1. IN MEMORIAM — Rev. GEOF. C. RYLY, M.A., Mus. Bac., Oxon.
2. TOCCATA — G. B. POLLERI.
3. OVERTURE from Epiphany — ALFRED KING, M.D.

Part 11, New Series.

1. PRELUDE AND FUGUE with POSTLUDE — E. A. CHAMBERLAYNE.
2. PRELUDE AND FUGUE — F. YOUNG.
3. FUGUE — ARCHIBALD DONALD.
4. FUGUE — WILLIAM HOPE.

Part 10, New Series.

1. FUGUE — ARCHIBALD DONALD.
2. PRELUDE AND FUGUE with POSTLUDE — E. A. CHAMBERLAYNE.
3. PRELUDE AND FUGUE — F. YOUNG.
   — SIR G. ELVEY.

Part 9, New Series.

1. ANDANTE CON MOTO — W. A MONTGOMERY, L.T.C.L.
2. FANTASIA in E minor — CUTHBERT HARRIS, Mus.B.,
3. POSTLUDE at Ephes. V. v. 19. Si tibi placeat, Mihi con displicet — W. CONRADI, (Y. of B. 1816). Org. St. Paul's Church, Schwerin i/m Germany,
4. HARVEST MARCH — HENRY J. POOLE.

Part 8, New Series.

1. SCHERZO MINUET — W. MULLINEUX, Organist of the Town Hall, Bolton.
2. INTRODUCTION to the Hymn on the Passion, "O Haupt Voll Blut und Wunden" — W. CONRADI. Organist Paul's Church, Schwerin, Germany,
3. THESIS AND ANTITHESIS, or DISPUTE, APPEASEMENT, CONCILIATION — W. CONRADI, Organist Paul's Church, Schwerin, Germany.
4. CARILLON in E — CUTHBERT HARRIS, Mus.B., F.R.C.O., &c.
5. ANDANTE "Hope" — INGLIS BERVON.
6. ORCHESTRAL MARCH in C — JAMES CRAPPER. L. Mus., Organist of the Parish Ch., Kirkcudbright.

Part 7, New Series.

1. ANDANTE GRAZIOSO in G — CHAS. E. MELVILLE, F.R.C.O.
2. POLISH SONG — CHOPIN. Arranged for the organ by PERCIVAL GARRETT.
3. INTRODUCTION, VARIATIONS, and FINALE on the Hymn Tune "Rockingham" CH. R. FISHER, Mus.B.
4. TWO SOFT MOVEMENTS — W. C. FILBY, I.S.M. 1. "Espérance." 2. "Tendresse."
5. ANDANTE in A flat — W GRIFFITH, Mus. B. Org. of St. Sepulchre Church, Northampton.
6. FUGUE, 4 Voice, 3 Subjects — DR. J. C. TILEY.

The Organist's Quarterly Journal (cont.).

Part 6, New Series.
Con Moto Moderato in C
    Orlando A. Mansfield, Mus.B., F.R.C.O.
2. Tempo di Menuetto - - - Geo. H. Ely.
3. Large in Memoriam, Reginald Adkins
    J. E. Adkins, F.R.C.O.
4. Andante in F - - - R. H. Heath.
5. Aberystwyth Offertoire - J. G. Mountford.
6. Andante in D (Prière) - E. Evelyn Barron, M.A.

Part 5, New Series.
1. Allegretto Scherzando in A flat W.E. Ashmall.
2. Andante Religioso in G - Dr. J. Bradford.
3. March Pomposo in E flat - Charles Darnton.
4. Andante Con Moto "Twilight"
    Ch. R. Fisher, Mus. B.
5. Minuet in F - - W. E. Belcher, F R.C.O.

Part 4, New Series.
1. Andante Moderato - - - F. Read.
2. Prelude and Fugue in D minor
    E. A. Chamberlayne.
3. Sketch - - - Arthur Geo. Colborn.
4. Fugue - - - James Turpin.
5. Allegro - - Charles H. Fisher.
6. Marche Mystique - - Theme by Roland
    de Lassus.—A Relic of Ancient Times.

Part 3, New Series.
1. Minuet and Trio in F.
    Ed. J. Bellerby, Mus. B., Oxon.
2. "Dundee" ("or French") - John P. Attwater.
3. Adagio. An Elegy, in G minor
    Chas. R. Fisher, Mus. B.
4. Andante. A major - - E. F. Horner
5. Allegro, D minor - - Geo. Minns (Ely

Part 2, New Series.
1. Toccata Fantasia (*Study in C minor*)
    E. T. Driffield.
2. Andante Grazioso - - W. Faulkes.
3. Marche Funebre - Arthur Wanderer.
4. Andante Semplice - E. A. Chamberlayne.
5. Festal March - - A. W. Ketelbey.

Part 1, New Series.
1. Offertoire in A minor - Fred. W. Dal (Leipzig).
2. Second Fantasia on Scotch Airs
    William Spark.
3. A little deles with Variations and Fugue)
    Charles Hunt.
4. Intermezzo - G. Townshend Driffield.

Part 103, July 1894.
1. Postlude in G Frederick W. Holloway, F.C.O
2. Suite: No. 1, Prelude; No. 2, Berceuse;
    No. 3, Toccata - Laurent Parodi (Genoa
3. Nocturne - - - William Lockett.
4. Andante Pastorale in B minor
    Jacob Bradford, Mus. D., Oxon.
5. Introductory Voluntary - Albert W. Ketelbey
6. Fugue - - - R. J. Rowe, L.R.A.M.

LONDON   WILLIAM REEVES, 83, CHARIN CROSS ROAD W.C

Books on Freemasonry

Published by W. REEVES, 83, Charing Cross Road, W.C.

12mo, red cloth, gilt, 323 pp., 3/6
Carlile (R.), Manual of Freemasonry, containing the First Three Degrees, The Royal Arch and Knights Templar Druids, The Degrees of Mark Man, Mark Master, Architect, Grand Architect., etc., etc.

12mo, blue cloth. gilt, 374 pp., 3/6
Fellows (J.), Mysteries of Freemasonry; or, An Exposition of the Religious Dogmas and Customs of the Ancient Egyptians; showing, from the origin, nature and objects of the rites and ceremonies of remote antiquity, their identity with the Order of Modern Masonry, with some remarks on the Metamorphosis of Apuleius, *with numerous illustrative woodcuts.*

12mo, green cloth, gilt, 254 pp., 3/6
Ritual and Illustrations of Freemasonry, *accompanied by very numerous engravings*, and a Key to the Phi Beta Kappa.

8vo, sewed, 26 pp. 1/-
Investigation into the Cause of the Hostility of the Church of Rome to Freemasonry, and an Inquiry into Freemasonry as it Was, and Is: with a Criticism as to how far the Order fulfils its Functions, by the Author of "The Text Book of Freemasonry."

Post 8vo, sewed, 48 pp., 1/-
Joachin and Boaz; or, an Authentic Key to the Door of Freemasonry, both Ancient and Modern

Post 8vo, sewed, 50 pp. 1/-
Three Distinct Knocks at the Door of the Most Ancient Freemasonry.

8vo, sewed, 1/-
The Origin of Freemasonry, or the 1717 Theory Exploded, by C. J. Paton, 8vo. 1s.

8vo, paper, 2/6 (post free 3/-)
Weisse (John A.), The Obelisk of Freemasonry, according to the Discoveries of Belzoni and Commander Gorringe: also Egyptian Symbols compared with those discovered in American Mounds.

Fifth thousand, 12mo, cloth 1/-
Pocket Lexicon of Freemasonry, by W. J. Morris, 18° P.D.D.G.M., St. Lawrence, District and Past Inspector Gen. Royal and Select Masters.

12mo, cloth, 62 pp., 2/-
Fox (T. L.), Freemaonry; An Account of the Early History of Freemasonry in England, with Illustrations of the Principles and Precepts advocated by that Institution.

Any of the above sent POST FREE *upon receipt of Remittance for price named.*

Books on Freemasonry

Published by W. REEVES,
83, Charing Cross Road, W.C.

12mo, blue cloth, red edges, 5/- (or calf limp, gilt edges, 10/6.)

Text Book of Freemasonry; a Complete Handbook of Instruction to all the Workings in the Various Mysteries and Ceremonies of CRAFT MASONRY, containing the Entered Apprentice, Fellow-craft, and Master Mason's degrees; the Ceremony of Installation of the W. Master and Officers of the Lodge, together with the whole of the Three Lectures; also the Ceremony of Exhaltation in the Supreme Order of the Holy Royal Arch, a Selection of Masonic Songs, etc., *illustrated with four engravings of the* **TRACING BOARDS**, by "A Member of the Craft," new and revised edition.

Ditto, Ditto, on thin paper, bound in leather pocket-book style, 5s.

The Three Tracing Boards, in 12mo, cloth line, 1s. 6d.

Ditto, **Larger Size**, roy. 8vo, 4 plates, 1s. 6d.

Post 8vo, cloth, 278 pp., 10/- (or crimson calf limp. gilt edges, 15/

Text Book of Advanced Freemasonry, containing for the self-Instruction of Candidates, the COMPLETE RITUALS of the HIGHER DEGREES, viz., Royal Ark Mariners, Mark Master, Royal Arch, Red Cross of Rome and Constantinople, Knights' Templar and Rose Croix de Heredom; also Monitorial Instructions on the 30th to the 33rd and last degree of Freemasonry, to which are added Historical Introductions and Explanatory remarks by the Author of the "Text Book."

8vo, cloth, 300 pp., 3/6

HONE (William), Ancient Mysteries described, especially the English Miracle Plays founded on the Apocryphal New Testament Story, extant among the unpublished MSS. in the British Museum, including notices of Ecclesiastical shows and Festivals of Fools and Asses, the English Boy Bishop Descent into Hell, the Lord Mayor's Show, the Guildhall Giants, Christmas Carols, etc., with engravings and Index

---

8vo, cloth, 3/6

HONE (William) The Apocryphal New Testament, being all the Gospels, Epistles and other pieces now extant attributed in the first four centuries to Jesus Christ, his Apostles and their Companions and not included in the New Testament by its compilers.

Any of the above sent POST FREE *upon receipt of Remittance for price named.*

www.ingramcontent.com/pod-product-compliance
Lightning Source LLC
Chambersburg PA
CBHW020304170426
43202CB00008B/486